87 New England Recipes for Home

By: Kelly Johnson

Table of Contents

Chicken Recipes:

- Clam Chowder
- Lobster Roll
- Boston Baked Beans
- New England Boiled Dinner
- Fisherman's Stew
- Indian Pudding
- Maple Glazed Salmon
- Apple Cider Doughnuts
- Boston Cream Pie
- Johnny Cakes
- Rhode Island Clam Cakes
- Scrod
- Pilgrim Sandwich
- Boston Brown Bread
- New England Pot Roast
- Apple Pie with Cheddar Cheese
- Cape Cod Cranberry Sauce
- Boston Cream Doughnuts
- Fish Chowder
- Blueberry Buckle
- Steamed Lobster
- Codfish Cakes
- Boston Cream Cupcakes
- Brown Bread Ice Cream
- New England Clam Dip
- Boiled Lobster Dinner
- Boston Baked Scrod
- Apple Cider Glazed Pork Chops
- Moxie Soda Pulled Pork
- New England Apple Cake
- Boston Brown Bread Muffins
- Maple Walnut Fudge
- New England Fried Clams
- Cranberry Walnut Bread
- Rhode Island Johnnycakes

- Baked Stuffed Lobster
- Anadama Bread
- Boston Cream Pie Cupcakes
- Cranberry Orange Muffins
- Maple Glazed Butternut Squash
- New England Seafood Bake
- Corn and Bacon Chowder
- Pumpkin Whoopie Pies
- New England Apple Cider Donut Holes
- Baked Beans with Maple Syrup
- Cape Codder Cocktail
- Grilled Swordfish Steaks
- Bluefish Pate
- New England Harvest Salad
- Apple Cider Chicken
- Cranberry Chutney
- Boston Cream Pie Trifle
- Lobster Bisque
- Maple Glazed Sweet Potatoes
- Blueberry Lemon Scones
- Boston Brown Bread Ice Cream Sandwiches
- Clam and COrn Fritters
- Boston Cream Pie Pancakes
- Cranberry Walnut Chicken Salad
- New England Pot Roast Sandwiches
- Maple Glazed Brussels Sprouts
- Chow Mein Sandwich
- Boston Cream Pie Martini
- Succotash
- Pumpkin Bisque
- New England Style Pancakes
- Clam and Corn Chowder
- Cranberry Glazed Ham
- Boston Cream Pie Cheesecake
- Lobster Newberg

Clam Chowder

Ingredients:

- 2 dozen fresh clams (or 2 cans of chopped clams)
- 4 slices bacon, chopped
- 1 onion, finely chopped
- 2 celery stalks, finely chopped
- 3 medium potatoes, peeled and diced
- 2 cups chicken broth
- 1 bay leaf
- 1 teaspoon dried thyme
- 1 cup heavy cream
- Salt and pepper to taste
- Fresh parsley for garnish

Instructions:

Prepare the Clams:
- If using fresh clams, scrub them thoroughly under cold water to remove any sand or debris. In a large pot, steam the clams with a small amount of water until they open. Discard any clams that do not open. Remove the clam meat from the shells and chop it coarsely. If using canned clams, drain and reserve the clam juice.

Cook Bacon and Vegetables:
- In a large soup pot over medium heat, cook the chopped bacon until it becomes crispy. Remove some bacon bits for garnish, leaving some in the pot. Add chopped onion and celery to the pot and sauté until they become softened.

Add Potatoes and Broth:
- Add the diced potatoes to the pot and stir well. Pour in the chicken broth, add the bay leaf and dried thyme. Bring the mixture to a simmer and cook until the potatoes are tender.

Combine Clams and Cream:
- Once the potatoes are cooked, add the chopped clams (fresh or canned) to the pot. If you used fresh clams, strain and add the reserved clam juice as well. Stir in the heavy cream, and let the chowder simmer for a few more minutes until heated through. Season with salt and pepper to taste.

Serve:

- Remove the bay leaf, and ladle the clam chowder into bowls. Garnish with the reserved crispy bacon bits and chopped fresh parsley.

Enjoy:
- Serve the clam chowder hot, perhaps with some oyster crackers or crusty bread on the side.

This New England Clam Chowder is rich, flavorful, and perfect for a comforting meal, especially during colder seasons. Adjust the seasoning according to your taste preferences.

Lobster Roll

Ingredients:

- 1 1/2 pounds cooked lobster meat, chopped into bite-sized pieces
- 1/2 cup mayonnaise
- 1-2 celery stalks, finely chopped
- 1-2 tablespoons fresh lemon juice
- Salt and pepper to taste
- 4-6 split-top hot dog rolls
- 2-3 tablespoons unsalted butter, melted
- Chopped fresh chives or parsley for garnish (optional)
- Lemon wedges for serving

Instructions:

Prepare the Lobster:
- If you haven't already, cook the lobster by boiling or steaming it. Once cooked, remove the meat from the shells and chop it into bite-sized pieces.

Make the Lobster Salad:
- In a bowl, combine the chopped lobster meat, mayonnaise, chopped celery, and fresh lemon juice. Gently toss the ingredients together until well combined. Season with salt and pepper to taste. Adjust the amount of mayonnaise according to your preference.

Butter and Toast the Rolls:
- Brush the outsides of the split-top hot dog rolls with melted butter. Toast them on a griddle or in a pan over medium heat until they are golden brown on both sides.

Fill the Rolls:
- Fill each toasted roll with a generous portion of the lobster salad mixture. The roll should be well-packed with the delicious lobster filling.

Garnish and Serve:
- Garnish the Lobster Rolls with chopped chives or parsley if desired. Serve the rolls immediately with lemon wedges on the side.

Enjoy:
- Enjoy your New England Lobster Rolls as a delightful and classic seafood treat!

Feel free to customize the recipe to your liking. Some variations may include adding a touch of Old Bay seasoning, using a different type of bread, or experimenting with additional herbs and spices in the lobster salad. The key is to let the fresh and sweet flavor of the lobster shine through.

Boston Baked Beans

Ingredients:

- 1 pound (about 2 cups) dried navy beans
- Water for soaking and cooking
- 1 large onion, finely chopped
- 1/2 cup molasses
- 1/4 cup brown sugar
- 2 teaspoons dry mustard
- 1/4 pound salt pork or bacon, diced
- 1 teaspoon salt
- 1/4 teaspoon black pepper
- 1/4 teaspoon ground cloves (optional)

Instructions:

Soak the Beans:
- Rinse the dried navy beans and remove any debris. Place the beans in a large bowl and cover them with water. Allow the beans to soak overnight. Alternatively, you can use a quick soak method by bringing the beans to a boil, then letting them sit for an hour before draining.

Preheat the Oven:
- Preheat your oven to 325°F (165°C).

Prepare the Beans:
- Drain the soaked beans and place them in a large pot. Cover the beans with water and bring them to a boil. Reduce the heat and simmer for about 10-15 minutes. Drain the beans.

Make the Sauce:
- In a separate bowl, mix together the molasses, brown sugar, dry mustard, salt, pepper, and ground cloves (if using). Stir until the ingredients are well combined.

Layer the Ingredients:
- In a bean pot or an oven-safe pot, layer the partially cooked beans, diced salt pork or bacon, and chopped onions. Repeat the layers until all ingredients are used.

Add the Sauce:
- Pour the prepared molasses and spice mixture over the layered beans and pork. Add enough water to just cover the beans.

Bake:

- Cover the pot and bake in the preheated oven for about 4-6 hours or until the beans are tender. Check the water level periodically and add more if necessary to keep the beans moist.

Serve:
- Once the beans are tender and the sauce has thickened, remove from the oven. Let the beans rest for a few minutes before serving.

Enjoy:
- Serve your Boston Baked Beans as a side dish alongside grilled meats, hot dogs, or simply on their own. They are a flavorful and hearty addition to any New England meal.

This traditional recipe captures the essence of Boston Baked Beans, offering a comforting and classic dish with a perfect balance of sweetness and smokiness. Adjust the seasoning according to your taste preferences.

New England Boiled Dinner

Ingredients:

- 3-4 pounds corned beef brisket
- 8-10 small red or Yukon Gold potatoes, halved
- 4-6 carrots, peeled and cut into chunks
- 1 small cabbage, cored and cut into wedges
- 1 onion, peeled and halved
- 2-3 cloves garlic, minced
- 1 bay leaf
- 10-12 whole black peppercorns
- Water (enough to cover the ingredients)
- Mustard or horseradish for serving (optional)

Instructions:

Prepare the Corned Beef:
- Rinse the corned beef under cold water to remove any excess brine. Place the corned beef in a large pot.

Add Vegetables:
- Add halved potatoes, carrot chunks, onion halves, minced garlic, bay leaf, and whole peppercorns to the pot with the corned beef.

Cover with Water:
- Pour enough water into the pot to cover all the ingredients. The water should fully submerge the meat and vegetables.

Simmer:
- Bring the water to a boil over high heat. Once boiling, reduce the heat to low, cover the pot, and let it simmer. Simmer for about 2.5 to 3 hours or until the corned beef is tender.

Add Cabbage:
- About 30 minutes before the corned beef is done, add the cabbage wedges to the pot. This ensures the cabbage cooks but doesn't become overly mushy.

Check Doneness:
- Test the doneness of the corned beef by inserting a fork into the meat. If it goes in easily, the corned beef is ready.

Serve:

- Remove the corned beef from the pot and let it rest for a few minutes before slicing. Arrange the sliced corned beef on a platter surrounded by the cooked vegetables.

Enjoy:
- Serve the New England Boiled Dinner with some of the cooking liquid spooned over the top. Optionally, serve with mustard or horseradish on the side.

This New England Boiled Dinner is a classic comfort food, perfect for family gatherings or a cozy meal on a chilly day. Adjust the cooking time based on the size of the corned beef and your desired level of tenderness.

Fisherman's Stew

Ingredients:

- 1 pound mixed seafood (such as shrimp, mussels, clams, and white fish fillets), cleaned and deveined
- 2 tablespoons olive oil
- 1 onion, finely chopped
- 2 cloves garlic, minced
- 1 red bell pepper, diced
- 1 fennel bulb, thinly sliced
- 1 celery stalk, diced
- 1 carrot, peeled and diced
- 1 can (14 ounces) diced tomatoes
- 1 cup fish or seafood broth
- 1 cup dry white wine
- 1 teaspoon dried thyme
- 1 bay leaf
- Salt and black pepper to taste
- Fresh parsley, chopped, for garnish
- Crusty bread for serving

Instructions:

Prepare Seafood:
- Clean and devein the shrimp, scrub the mussels and clams, and cut the white fish fillets into bite-sized pieces. Set aside.

Sauté Aromatics:
- In a large pot or Dutch oven, heat olive oil over medium heat. Add chopped onion, minced garlic, diced bell pepper, sliced fennel, diced celery, and diced carrot. Sauté for about 5-7 minutes or until the vegetables are softened.

Add Tomatoes and Broth:
- Add the diced tomatoes (with their juices) to the pot. Pour in the fish or seafood broth and dry white wine. Stir well to combine.

Season and Simmer:
- Add dried thyme, a bay leaf, salt, and black pepper to the pot. Bring the mixture to a simmer and let it cook for about 15-20 minutes to allow the flavors to meld.

Add Seafood:
- Add the mixed seafood to the pot. Simmer for an additional 5-7 minutes or until the seafood is cooked through. Discard any unopened mussels or clams.

Adjust Seasoning:
- Taste the stew and adjust the seasoning if necessary, adding more salt and pepper to taste.

Serve:
- Ladle the Fisherman's Stew into bowls, garnish with chopped fresh parsley, and serve with crusty bread on the side.

Enjoy:
- Enjoy this delicious Fisherman's Stew, savoring the rich flavors of the sea and the comforting combination of vegetables and broth.

Feel free to customize the seafood choices based on your preferences and what's available. This Fisherman's Stew is perfect for a cozy dinner, especially during colder months when a warm and flavorful soup is especially satisfying.

Indian Pudding

Ingredients:

- 1/2 cup cornmeal
- 2 cups milk
- 1/2 cup molasses
- 1/4 cup unsalted butter
- 1/2 teaspoon salt
- 1/2 teaspoon ground cinnamon
- 1/4 teaspoon ground ginger
- 1/4 teaspoon ground nutmeg
- 1/4 cup brown sugar
- 2 large eggs, beaten
- 1 teaspoon vanilla extract
- Whipped cream or vanilla ice cream for serving (optional)

Instructions:

Preheat the Oven:
- Preheat your oven to 325°F (163°C).

Combine Cornmeal and Milk:
- In a medium-sized saucepan, whisk together the cornmeal and milk. Cook over medium heat, stirring constantly until the mixture thickens. This usually takes about 5-7 minutes.

Add Molasses and Butter:
- Add molasses, unsalted butter, salt, cinnamon, ginger, and nutmeg to the cornmeal mixture. Continue to cook and stir until the butter is melted and the ingredients are well combined.

Add Brown Sugar:
- Stir in the brown sugar until it dissolves in the mixture.

Temper the Eggs:
- In a separate bowl, beat the eggs. Take a small amount of the hot cornmeal mixture and gradually whisk it into the beaten eggs. This helps to temper the eggs, preventing them from scrambling when added to the hot mixture.

Combine Mixtures:
- Gradually add the tempered eggs back into the saucepan, stirring continuously to avoid lumps.

Add Vanilla:
- Stir in the vanilla extract.

Bake:
- Pour the mixture into a greased baking dish. Bake in the preheated oven for approximately 1.5 to 2 hours or until the pudding is set and has a firm consistency.

Serve:
- Allow the Indian Pudding to cool for a bit before serving. It's traditionally served warm. You can top it with whipped cream or a scoop of vanilla ice cream if desired.

Enjoy:
- Enjoy the warm and comforting flavors of Indian Pudding, a classic New England dessert.

Indian Pudding has a unique texture and flavor, combining the sweetness of molasses with the warmth of spices. It's a delightful treat, especially during colder seasons.

Maple Glazed Salmon

Ingredients:

- 4 salmon fillets (about 6 ounces each), skin-on or skinless
- Salt and black pepper to taste
- 2 tablespoons olive oil

For the Maple Glaze:

- 1/4 cup pure maple syrup
- 2 tablespoons soy sauce (or tamari for a gluten-free option)
- 1 tablespoon Dijon mustard
- 1 tablespoon rice vinegar or apple cider vinegar
- 1 teaspoon minced garlic
- 1 teaspoon grated fresh ginger
- Pinch of red pepper flakes (optional for a hint of heat)
- Chopped fresh parsley or green onions for garnish (optional)

Instructions:

Preheat the Oven:
- Preheat your oven to 400°F (200°C).

Season Salmon:
- Pat the salmon fillets dry with a paper towel. Season both sides with salt and black pepper.

Sear Salmon:
- In an oven-safe skillet, heat olive oil over medium-high heat. Place the salmon fillets in the skillet, skin-side down if they have skin. Sear for 2-3 minutes until the edges are golden brown.

Prepare Maple Glaze:
- While the salmon is searing, in a small bowl, whisk together maple syrup, soy sauce, Dijon mustard, rice vinegar, minced garlic, grated ginger, and red pepper flakes if using.

Glaze Salmon:
- Pour the maple glaze over the seared salmon fillets. Use a brush to evenly coat the salmon with the glaze.

Bake:

- Transfer the skillet to the preheated oven and bake for about 10-12 minutes or until the salmon is cooked through. The internal temperature should reach 145°F (63°C).

Broil (Optional):
- If you'd like to add a caramelized finish, you can broil the salmon for an additional 1-2 minutes, keeping a close eye to prevent burning.

Garnish and Serve:
- Remove the skillet from the oven, garnish the salmon with chopped fresh parsley or green onions if desired, and serve immediately.

Enjoy:
- Enjoy the succulent and flavorful Maple Glazed Salmon, perfect with sides like roasted vegetables, rice, or a fresh salad.

This Maple Glazed Salmon recipe provides a perfect balance of sweet and savory flavors, making it a delightful choice for a quick and impressive meal. Adjust the sweetness and seasoning according to your taste preferences.

Apple Cider Doughnuts

Ingredients:

For the Doughnuts:

- 2 cups apple cider
- 2 cups all-purpose flour
- 1 1/2 teaspoons baking powder
- 1/2 teaspoon baking soda
- 1/2 teaspoon ground cinnamon
- 1/4 teaspoon ground nutmeg
- 1/4 teaspoon salt
- 1/2 cup unsalted butter, softened
- 1/2 cup granulated sugar
- 1/2 cup packed brown sugar
- 2 large eggs
- 1 teaspoon vanilla extract

For Rolling:

- 1/2 cup granulated sugar
- 1 teaspoon ground cinnamon

Instructions:

Reduce Apple Cider:
- In a saucepan over medium heat, reduce the apple cider to 1/2 cup. Allow it to cool to room temperature.

Preheat the Oven:
- Preheat your oven to 350°F (175°C). Grease two standard doughnut pans.

Whisk Dry Ingredients:
- In a medium bowl, whisk together the flour, baking powder, baking soda, ground cinnamon, ground nutmeg, and salt.

Cream Butter and Sugars:
- In a separate large bowl, cream together the softened butter, granulated sugar, and brown sugar until light and fluffy.

Add Eggs and Vanilla:

- Add the eggs one at a time, beating well after each addition. Stir in the vanilla extract.

Combine Wet and Dry Ingredients:
- Gradually add the dry ingredients to the wet ingredients, alternating with the reduced apple cider. Begin and end with the dry ingredients. Mix until just combined.

Fill Doughnut Pans:
- Spoon or pipe the batter into the prepared doughnut pans, filling each cavity about 2/3 full.

Bake:
- Bake in the preheated oven for 12-15 minutes or until a toothpick inserted into a doughnut comes out clean.

Roll in Cinnamon Sugar:
- While the doughnuts are baking, mix together the granulated sugar and ground cinnamon in a shallow bowl. Once the doughnuts are cool enough to handle, but still warm, roll each doughnut in the cinnamon sugar mixture to coat.

Enjoy:
- Serve the Apple Cider Doughnuts warm and enjoy the wonderful flavors of fall!

These Apple Cider Doughnuts are a perfect way to celebrate the autumn season. The combination of apple cider and warm spices makes them a delicious and comforting treat.

Boston Cream Pie

Ingredients:

For the Sponge Cake:

- 1 cup all-purpose flour
- 1 teaspoon baking powder
- 1/4 teaspoon salt
- 4 large eggs, room temperature
- 1 cup granulated sugar
- 1/2 cup unsalted butter, melted
- 1/2 cup whole milk
- 1 teaspoon vanilla extract

For the Pastry Cream:

- 2 cups whole milk
- 1/2 cup granulated sugar
- 1/4 cup cornstarch
- 1/4 teaspoon salt
- 4 large egg yolks
- 2 tablespoons unsalted butter
- 1 teaspoon vanilla extract

For the Chocolate Ganache:

- 6 ounces semisweet or bittersweet chocolate, finely chopped
- 1/2 cup heavy cream

Instructions:

Preheat the Oven:
- Preheat your oven to 350°F (175°C). Grease and flour two 9-inch round cake pans.

Make the Sponge Cake:
- In a bowl, whisk together the flour, baking powder, and salt. In another bowl, beat the eggs with an electric mixer until they become thick and pale. Gradually add the sugar and continue to beat until the mixture is well combined. Add the melted butter, milk, and vanilla extract, and mix until

smooth. Gradually add the dry ingredients and mix until just combined. Divide the batter between the prepared cake pans.

Bake:
- Bake in the preheated oven for 20-25 minutes or until a toothpick inserted into the center of the cakes comes out clean. Allow the cakes to cool in the pans for 10 minutes, then transfer them to a wire rack to cool completely.

Make the Pastry Cream:
- In a saucepan, heat the milk until it just begins to simmer. In a separate bowl, whisk together the sugar, cornstarch, and salt. Add the egg yolks to the sugar mixture and whisk until well combined. Gradually pour the hot milk into the egg mixture, whisking constantly. Return the mixture to the saucepan and cook over medium heat, whisking constantly, until it thickens. Remove from heat, stir in the butter and vanilla extract. Cover the surface of the pastry cream with plastic wrap to prevent a skin from forming. Allow it to cool to room temperature.

Assemble the Cake:
- Place one of the sponge cakes on a serving plate. Spread the cooled pastry cream evenly over the top. Place the second sponge cake on top.

Make the Chocolate Ganache:
- In a heatproof bowl, place the chopped chocolate. In a small saucepan, heat the cream until it just begins to simmer. Pour the hot cream over the chocolate and let it sit for a minute. Stir until the chocolate is completely melted and the mixture is smooth.

Finish the Cake:
- Pour the chocolate ganache over the top of the assembled cake, allowing it to drip down the sides. Use a spatula to smooth the ganache on the top.

Chill:
- Refrigerate the Boston Cream Pie for at least 2 hours before serving to allow the ganache to set.

Enjoy:
- Slice and enjoy this classic Boston Cream Pie with its delightful layers of sponge cake, pastry cream, and chocolate ganache.

This Boston Cream Pie recipe captures the timeless and irresistible combination of flavors and textures that make it a favorite dessert.

Johnny Cakes

Ingredients:

- 1 cup cornmeal
- 1 cup all-purpose flour
- 2 tablespoons sugar
- 1 teaspoon baking powder
- 1/2 teaspoon baking soda
- 1/2 teaspoon salt
- 1 1/2 cups buttermilk
- 1 large egg
- 2 tablespoons melted butter or vegetable oil
- Butter or oil for cooking (for greasing the griddle or pan)
- Maple syrup or honey for serving

Instructions:

Preheat the Griddle or Pan:
- Preheat a griddle or non-stick skillet over medium heat. Lightly grease it with butter or oil.

Prepare the Dry Ingredients:
- In a large mixing bowl, whisk together the cornmeal, all-purpose flour, sugar, baking powder, baking soda, and salt.

Combine Wet Ingredients:
- In a separate bowl, whisk together the buttermilk, egg, and melted butter or oil.

Mix the Batter:
- Pour the wet ingredients into the dry ingredients and stir until just combined. The batter should be slightly lumpy.

Cook the Johnny Cakes:
- Spoon the batter onto the preheated griddle or skillet to form small pancakes. Cook until bubbles form on the surface, and the edges begin to look set, then flip and cook the other side until golden brown.

Keep Warm:
- Transfer the cooked Johnny Cakes to a plate and cover with a kitchen towel to keep them warm while cooking the remaining batter.

Serve:
- Serve the Johnny Cakes warm with a drizzle of maple syrup or honey.

Enjoy:
- Enjoy these delicious cornmeal pancakes as a side dish for savory meals or as a breakfast treat.

Johnny Cakes are versatile and can be enjoyed in various ways. They can be served with savory toppings like butter, cheese, or even salsa, or enjoyed sweet with syrup, honey, or fruit compote. Their simplicity makes them a classic comfort food that can be adapted to suit your taste preferences.

Rhode Island Clam Cakes

Ingredients:

- 1 cup all-purpose flour
- 1 cup cornmeal
- 1 teaspoon baking powder
- 1/2 teaspoon salt
- 1/4 teaspoon black pepper
- 1/2 cup milk
- 1/2 cup clam juice (reserved from canned clams or freshly steamed clams)
- 1 large egg
- 1 cup chopped clams (canned or steamed and chopped)
- Vegetable oil for frying
- Lemon wedges for serving (optional)
- Tartar sauce or cocktail sauce for dipping (optional)

Instructions:

Prepare Clams:
- If using canned clams, drain and reserve the clam juice. If using fresh clams, steam them until they open. Discard any unopened clams, and chop the clam meat.

Make the Batter:
- In a large mixing bowl, whisk together the flour, cornmeal, baking powder, salt, and black pepper.

Add Wet Ingredients:
- In a separate bowl, whisk together the milk, clam juice, and egg.

Combine Ingredients:
- Pour the wet ingredients into the dry ingredients and stir until just combined. Fold in the chopped clams.

Heat Oil:
- In a deep fryer or a heavy-bottomed pot, heat vegetable oil to 350°F (175°C).

Drop and Fry:
- Using a spoon or an ice cream scoop, drop spoonfuls of the batter into the hot oil. Fry the clam cakes until they are golden brown and cooked through, about 2-3 minutes per side.

Drain and Serve:

- Remove the clam cakes from the oil and drain them on paper towels to absorb excess oil.

Serve:
- Serve Rhode Island Clam Cakes warm, optionally with lemon wedges and your choice of tartar sauce or cocktail sauce for dipping.

Enjoy:
- Enjoy these crispy and savory Rhode Island Clam Cakes as a delightful snack or appetizer, perfect for sharing.

Rhode Island Clam Cakes are a quintessential summer treat in the region and are often enjoyed with other seafood dishes or as a standalone snack. Adjust the seasoning and dipping sauce according to your preferences.

Scrod

Baked Scrod with Lemon and Herbs:

Ingredients:

- 4 scrod fillets (about 6 ounces each)
- 2 tablespoons olive oil
- 2 tablespoons fresh lemon juice
- 2 cloves garlic, minced
- 1 teaspoon dried thyme (or 1 tablespoon fresh thyme)
- 1 teaspoon dried oregano (or 1 tablespoon fresh oregano)
- Salt and black pepper to taste
- Lemon wedges for serving
- Fresh parsley for garnish (optional)

Instructions:

Preheat the Oven:
- Preheat your oven to 400°F (200°C).

Prepare the Scrod:
- Pat the scrod fillets dry with paper towels. Place them in a baking dish.

Make the Marinade:
- In a small bowl, whisk together olive oil, lemon juice, minced garlic, thyme, oregano, salt, and black pepper.

Marinate the Scrod:
- Pour the marinade over the scrod fillets, ensuring they are well coated. Allow them to marinate for about 15-20 minutes.

Bake:
- Bake the scrod in the preheated oven for approximately 12-15 minutes or until the fish is opaque and flakes easily with a fork.

Broil (Optional):
- For a golden crust, you can broil the scrod for an additional 1-2 minutes at the end of the cooking time, keeping a close eye to prevent burning.

Serve:
- Remove the baked scrod from the oven and transfer the fillets to serving plates. Drizzle any remaining juices from the baking dish over the top.

Garnish and Enjoy:

- Garnish with fresh parsley if desired and serve with lemon wedges on the side. This baked scrod is delicious when paired with steamed vegetables, rice, or a simple green salad.

This recipe highlights the natural flavors of the scrod with a burst of citrus and herbs. Adjust the seasoning and herbs to your taste preferences, and feel free to customize the dish with your favorite sides.

Pilgrim Sandwich

Ingredients:

- Sliced turkey (roasted or leftover from Thanksgiving)
- Stuffing (homemade or store-bought)
- Cranberry sauce
- Mayonnaise
- Sliced bread or rolls

Instructions:

Prepare Ingredients:
- If you don't have leftover turkey, roast or slice some turkey breast. Warm up or prepare the stuffing according to the package or your preferred recipe. Ensure you have cranberry sauce and mayonnaise ready.

Assemble the Sandwich:
- Lay out slices of bread or open rolls on a clean surface.

Layer the Turkey:
- Place a generous portion of sliced turkey on the bottom half of the bread or roll.

Add Stuffing:
- Spoon some stuffing over the turkey layer. Ensure an even distribution across the sandwich.

Top with Cranberry Sauce:
- Add a layer of cranberry sauce over the stuffing. This brings a sweet and tangy flavor to balance the savory turkey and stuffing.

Spread Mayonnaise:
- Spread a layer of mayonnaise on the top half of the bread or roll. This adds creaminess to the sandwich.

Assemble and Slice:
- Place the top half of the bread or roll over the layers to close the sandwich. If you're using a roll, you can secure it with toothpicks or wrap it in parchment paper.

Serve:
- Serve the Pilgrim Sandwich immediately, or wrap it for later. You can also slice it in half diagonally for a visually appealing presentation.

Enjoy:

- Enjoy the Pilgrim Sandwich, savoring the combination of Thanksgiving flavors in each bite.

Feel free to customize the Pilgrim Sandwich to your liking. Some variations include adding a slice of cheese, using leftover mashed potatoes, or incorporating other favorite Thanksgiving sides. It's a creative and delicious way to enjoy the flavors of the holiday in a convenient and portable form.

Boston Brown Bread

Ingredients:

- 1 cup cornmeal
- 1 cup whole wheat flour
- 1 cup rye flour
- 1 teaspoon baking soda
- 1/2 teaspoon salt
- 3/4 cup molasses
- 1 cup buttermilk
- 1/2 cup raisins or currants (optional)

Instructions:

Prepare Steaming Equipment:
- Grease a 1-quart heatproof bowl or a series of smaller heatproof bowls. You'll need a large pot with a tight-fitting lid for steaming.

Mix Dry Ingredients:
- In a large mixing bowl, combine the cornmeal, whole wheat flour, rye flour, baking soda, and salt. If you're using raisins or currants, add them to the dry mixture.

Combine Wet Ingredients:
- In a separate bowl, whisk together the molasses and buttermilk.

Combine Wet and Dry Ingredients:
- Pour the wet ingredients into the dry ingredients and stir until just combined. The batter will be thick.

Fill the Bowl(s):
- Pour the batter into the greased bowl(s), leaving about an inch of space at the top to allow for expansion.

Cover and Steam:
- Cover the bowl(s) tightly with aluminum foil or a lid. Place them in a large pot and add enough water to come about halfway up the sides of the bowl(s). Bring the water to a boil, then reduce the heat to a simmer. Steam the bread for 2 to 2.5 hours, checking occasionally and adding more water if needed.

Check for Doneness:
- Insert a toothpick into the center of the bread; if it comes out clean, the bread is done.

Cool and Serve:
- Allow the Boston Brown Bread to cool for a few minutes before removing it from the bowl. Run a knife around the edges to loosen it. Invert the bowl to release the bread. Let it cool completely before slicing.

Slice and Enjoy:
- Slice the Boston Brown Bread and serve it with butter, cream cheese, or your favorite spread.

This steamed Boston Brown Bread has a unique texture and flavor, making it a distinctive and delicious addition to your New England-inspired meals.

New England Pot Roast

Ingredients:

- 3-4 pounds beef chuck roast
- Salt and black pepper to taste
- 2 tablespoons vegetable oil
- 2 onions, sliced
- 4 carrots, peeled and cut into chunks
- 4 potatoes, peeled and cut into chunks
- 2 cloves garlic, minced
- 2 cups beef broth
- 1 cup red wine (or additional beef broth)
- 1 tablespoon tomato paste
- 1 teaspoon dried thyme
- 1 teaspoon dried rosemary
- 2 bay leaves

Instructions:

Preheat the Oven:
- Preheat your oven to 325°F (163°C).

Season and Brown the Roast:
- Season the beef chuck roast with salt and black pepper. In a large oven-safe pot or Dutch oven, heat vegetable oil over medium-high heat. Brown the roast on all sides to develop a rich flavor. Remove the roast from the pot and set it aside.

Sauté Vegetables:
- In the same pot, add sliced onions, carrots, and potatoes. Sauté for about 5 minutes until the vegetables start to soften. Add minced garlic and sauté for an additional minute.

Deglaze the Pot:
- Pour in the red wine (or beef broth) to deglaze the pot, scraping up any browned bits from the bottom.

Add Remaining Ingredients:
- Return the browned roast to the pot. Add beef broth, tomato paste, dried thyme, dried rosemary, and bay leaves.

Bring to a Simmer:

- Bring the liquid to a simmer. Once simmering, cover the pot with a lid.

Transfer to Oven:
- Transfer the covered pot to the preheated oven. Allow the roast to cook for about 2.5 to 3 hours or until the meat is fork-tender.

Check Doneness:
- Check the roast for doneness. The meat should be easy to shred with a fork.

Serve:
- Remove the bay leaves and discard them. Shred the beef into chunks and serve it with the vegetables, spooning some of the flavorful broth over the top.

Enjoy:
- Enjoy this New England Pot Roast with its rich and savory flavors. It's a comforting dish, perfect for cooler weather.

Feel free to customize the recipe by adding other vegetables like celery or mushrooms.

The slow cooking process allows the flavors to meld, resulting in a deliciously tender pot roast.

Apple Pie with Cheddar Cheese

Ingredients:

For the Pie Crust:

- 2 1/2 cups all-purpose flour
- 1 cup unsalted butter, cold and cubed
- 1/2 teaspoon salt
- 1 cup sharp cheddar cheese, shredded
- 6-8 tablespoons ice water

For the Apple Filling:

- 6-7 cups tart apples (such as Granny Smith), peeled, cored, and sliced
- 3/4 cup granulated sugar
- 1/4 cup light brown sugar, packed
- 1 tablespoon lemon juice
- 1 teaspoon ground cinnamon
- 1/4 teaspoon ground nutmeg
- 1/4 teaspoon salt
- 2 tablespoons all-purpose flour

For Assembly:

- 1 tablespoon unsalted butter, cut into small pieces
- Egg wash (1 egg beaten with 1 tablespoon water)
- Granulated sugar for sprinkling (optional)

Instructions:

Prepare the Pie Crust:

> In a food processor, pulse together the flour and salt.
> Add the cold, cubed butter and shredded cheddar cheese. Pulse until the mixture resembles coarse crumbs.
> Gradually add ice water, one tablespoon at a time, pulsing until the dough comes together.
> Divide the dough in half, shape each half into a disc, wrap in plastic wrap, and refrigerate for at least 1 hour.

Prepare the Apple Filling:

> In a large bowl, combine the sliced apples, granulated sugar, brown sugar, lemon juice, ground cinnamon, ground nutmeg, salt, and flour. Toss until the apples are evenly coated. Let it sit for about 15-20 minutes.

Assemble the Pie:

> Preheat the oven to 400°F (200°C).
> Roll out one disc of chilled pie dough on a floured surface to fit a 9-inch pie dish. Transfer the dough to the pie dish.
> Fill the crust with the prepared apple filling, spreading it evenly.
> Dot the filling with small pieces of unsalted butter.
> Roll out the second disc of pie dough and place it over the filling. Trim the excess dough and crimp the edges to seal.
> Cut a few slits on the top crust to allow steam to escape.
> Optionally, brush the top crust with the egg wash and sprinkle with granulated sugar for a golden finish.
> Place the pie on a baking sheet to catch any drips and bake in the preheated oven for about 45-50 minutes or until the crust is golden brown and the filling is bubbly.
> Allow the pie to cool before serving.

Serve and Enjoy:

Slice and serve the Apple Pie with Cheddar Cheese on its own or with a scoop of vanilla ice cream. The combination of the sweet apple filling and the savory cheddar cheese crust creates a deliciously balanced dessert.

Cape Cod Cranberry Sauce

Ingredients:

- 12 ounces fresh cranberries, rinsed and picked over
- 1 cup granulated sugar
- 1 cup orange juice
- Zest of 1 orange
- 1/2 cup water
- 1 cinnamon stick
- 1/4 teaspoon ground cloves

Instructions:

Combine Ingredients:
- In a medium-sized saucepan, combine the fresh cranberries, granulated sugar, orange juice, orange zest, water, cinnamon stick, and ground cloves.

Bring to a Boil:
- Bring the mixture to a boil over medium-high heat, stirring occasionally.

Simmer:
- Reduce the heat to low and let the cranberry sauce simmer. Allow it to cook for about 10-15 minutes or until the cranberries burst and the sauce thickens. Stir occasionally.

Adjust Sweetness:
- Taste the cranberry sauce and adjust the sweetness if necessary. Add more sugar if you prefer it sweeter.

Remove Cinnamon Stick:
- Once the cranberry sauce has reached your desired consistency, remove the cinnamon stick.

Cool and Serve:
- Allow the cranberry sauce to cool to room temperature. It will continue to thicken as it cools.

Refrigerate:
- Refrigerate the cranberry sauce until it's ready to be served. It can be made ahead of time and stored in the refrigerator.

Serve:
- Serve the Cape Cod Cranberry Sauce as a side dish with turkey, chicken, or any holiday meal. It also pairs well with cheese, sandwiches, and more.

Enjoy:
- Enjoy the burst of flavors from the tart cranberries, citrusy orange, and warm spices in this Cape Cod-inspired cranberry sauce.

Feel free to customize the recipe by adding chopped nuts, grated ginger, or a splash of cranberry liqueur for an extra layer of flavor. This homemade cranberry sauce is a wonderful addition to your holiday table and brings a taste of Cape Cod to your celebrations.

Boston Cream Doughnuts

Ingredients:

For the Doughnuts:

- 2 1/4 teaspoons (1 packet) active dry yeast
- 1 cup warm milk (about 110°F or 43°C)
- 1/4 cup granulated sugar
- 3 1/2 cups all-purpose flour
- 1/2 teaspoon salt
- 1/4 teaspoon ground nutmeg
- 1/4 cup unsalted butter, softened
- 2 large eggs

For the Custard Filling:

- 2 cups whole milk
- 1/2 cup granulated sugar
- 1/4 cup cornstarch
- 1/4 teaspoon salt
- 4 large egg yolks
- 2 tablespoons unsalted butter
- 1 teaspoon vanilla extract

For the Chocolate Glaze:

- 1/2 cup heavy cream
- 1 cup semisweet chocolate chips
- 1 tablespoon unsalted butter
- 1 teaspoon vanilla extract

Instructions:

Prepare the Dough:

> In a small bowl, combine the warm milk, sugar, and yeast. Let it sit for about 5-10 minutes until foamy.
> In a large mixing bowl or the bowl of a stand mixer, combine the flour, salt, and nutmeg.

Add the yeast mixture, softened butter, and eggs to the dry ingredients. Mix until the dough comes together.

Knead the dough on a floured surface or in the stand mixer until it becomes smooth and elastic. Place the dough in a greased bowl, cover it with a damp cloth, and let it rise in a warm place for about 1-1.5 hours or until doubled in size.

Roll out the dough on a floured surface to about 1/2-inch thickness. Cut out doughnuts using a round cutter.

Place the cut doughnuts on a baking sheet, cover with a cloth, and let them rise for another 30-45 minutes.

Heat oil in a deep fryer or large, deep pot to 350°F (175°C). Fry the doughnuts until golden brown on both sides. Remove and place on a paper towel-lined plate to drain excess oil.

Prepare the Custard Filling:

In a saucepan, heat the milk until it just begins to simmer.

In a bowl, whisk together sugar, cornstarch, salt, and egg yolks until smooth.

Gradually pour the hot milk into the egg mixture, whisking constantly.

Return the mixture to the saucepan and cook over medium heat, whisking constantly, until it thickens.

Remove from heat, stir in butter and vanilla extract. Let the custard cool.

Fill the Doughnuts:

Once the doughnuts have cooled, use a piping bag to fill them with the custard. You can make a small hole in each doughnut using a skewer or a piping tip.

Prepare the Chocolate Glaze:

In a saucepan, heat the cream until it just begins to simmer.

Pour the hot cream over the chocolate chips and butter. Let it sit for a minute, then stir until smooth.

Stir in vanilla extract.

Glaze the Doughnuts:

Dip the filled doughnuts into the chocolate glaze, allowing excess to drip off.

Place the glazed doughnuts on a wire rack to set.

Enjoy your homemade Boston Cream Doughnuts!

These Boston Cream Doughnuts are a delightful treat with a perfect balance of soft dough, creamy custard, and rich chocolate glaze.

Fish Chowder

Ingredients:

- 1 1/2 pounds white fish fillets (such as cod or haddock), cut into bite-sized pieces
- 3 tablespoons unsalted butter
- 1 onion, finely chopped
- 2 celery stalks, diced
- 2 carrots, peeled and diced
- 3 cloves garlic, minced
- 3 tablespoons all-purpose flour
- 4 cups fish or vegetable broth
- 3 cups potatoes, peeled and diced
- 1 bay leaf
- 1 teaspoon dried thyme
- Salt and black pepper to taste
- 2 cups whole milk or half-and-half
- Fresh parsley, chopped, for garnish

Instructions:

Prepare Fish:
- Cut the fish fillets into bite-sized pieces and set aside.

Sauté Vegetables:
- In a large pot or Dutch oven, melt the butter over medium heat. Add chopped onions, diced celery, and diced carrots. Sauté until the vegetables are softened, about 5 minutes.

Add Garlic and Flour:
- Add minced garlic and cook for an additional 1-2 minutes. Sprinkle the flour over the vegetables and stir well to coat.

Pour in Broth:
- Gradually pour in the fish or vegetable broth, stirring constantly to avoid lumps. Bring the mixture to a simmer.

Add Potatoes and Seasonings:
- Add diced potatoes, bay leaf, dried thyme, salt, and black pepper to the pot. Stir well and let it simmer for about 15-20 minutes or until the potatoes are tender.

Add Fish:

- Gently add the fish pieces to the pot. Simmer for an additional 5-7 minutes or until the fish is cooked through and flakes easily.

Pour in Milk:
- Pour in the whole milk or half-and-half, stirring constantly. Heat the chowder until it's warmed through, but do not let it boil.

Adjust Seasoning:
- Taste the chowder and adjust the seasoning if needed. Remove the bay leaf.

Serve:
- Ladle the Fish Chowder into bowls. Garnish with chopped fresh parsley.

Enjoy:
- Enjoy the comforting and creamy Fish Chowder with crusty bread or oyster crackers.

This Fish Chowder is a wonderful dish that highlights the flavors of the sea. It's perfect for warming up on a chilly day and makes for a satisfying meal.

Blueberry Buckle

Ingredients:

For the Cake:

- 2 cups all-purpose flour
- 2 teaspoons baking powder
- 1/2 teaspoon salt
- 1/2 cup unsalted butter, softened
- 3/4 cup granulated sugar
- 2 large eggs
- 1 teaspoon vanilla extract
- 1/2 cup milk
- 2 cups fresh or frozen blueberries (if using frozen, do not thaw)

For the Streusel Topping:

- 1/2 cup granulated sugar
- 1/3 cup all-purpose flour
- 1/2 teaspoon ground cinnamon
- 1/4 cup unsalted butter, softened

Instructions:

Preheat the Oven:
- Preheat your oven to 375°F (190°C). Grease and flour a 9-inch square baking pan.

Prepare the Streusel Topping:
- In a small bowl, combine the sugar, flour, and ground cinnamon for the streusel topping. Cut in the softened butter using a fork or your fingers until the mixture resembles coarse crumbs. Set aside.

Make the Cake Batter:
- In a medium bowl, whisk together the flour, baking powder, and salt.

Cream Butter and Sugar:
- In a large mixing bowl, cream together the softened butter and granulated sugar until light and fluffy.

Add Eggs and Vanilla:

- Add the eggs one at a time, beating well after each addition. Stir in the vanilla extract.

Alternate Flour and Milk:
- Gradually add the dry ingredients to the wet ingredients, alternating with the milk. Begin and end with the dry ingredients, mixing until just combined.

Fold in Blueberries:
- Gently fold in the blueberries until evenly distributed throughout the batter.

Assemble in Pan:
- Spread the batter evenly into the prepared baking pan.

Add Streusel Topping:
- Sprinkle the streusel topping over the batter, covering it evenly.

Bake:
- Bake in the preheated oven for 40-45 minutes or until a toothpick inserted into the center comes out clean, and the top is golden brown.

Cool:
- Allow the Blueberry Buckle to cool in the pan on a wire rack.

Serve:
- Once cooled, cut into squares and serve. You can enjoy it as is or with a scoop of vanilla ice cream for an extra treat.

Enjoy:
- Enjoy the moist and delicious Blueberry Buckle with its irresistible blueberry-studded cake and crumbly streusel topping.

This Blueberry Buckle recipe is a wonderful way to showcase the flavor of fresh blueberries. Whether served as a dessert or a sweet breakfast treat, it's sure to be a hit with blueberry lovers.

Steamed Lobster

Ingredients:

- Live lobsters
- Water
- Salt

Equipment:

- Large pot with a tight-fitting lid or a lobster steamer pot

Instructions:

    Prepare the Lobsters:
- Choose live lobsters for the freshest taste. Check for lively movement and make sure they are not lethargic. Rinse them under cold water.

    Fill the Pot:
- Fill a large pot with enough water to cover the lobsters. Add a generous amount of salt to the water. Aim for about 2-3 tablespoons of salt per gallon of water.

    Boil Water:
- Bring the salted water to a rolling boil.

    Insert Lobsters:
- Carefully place the live lobsters into the boiling water. Be cautious, as they may be quite active.

    Cover and Steam:
- Immediately cover the pot with a tight-fitting lid. Reduce the heat slightly to maintain a vigorous simmer, but not a rolling boil. Steam the lobsters for about 8-10 minutes for the first pound, and add 3 minutes for each additional pound. For example, a 2-pound lobster would steam for about 11-13 minutes.

    Check Doneness:
- The lobsters are done when they turn a bright red color, and the antennae can be easily pulled off. The internal temperature should reach 140°F (60°C).

    Remove and Serve:

- Use tongs to carefully remove the lobsters from the pot. Allow them to drain for a moment, and then serve immediately.

Crack and Enjoy:
- Use lobster crackers or kitchen shears to crack open the lobster shells. Serve with melted butter, lemon wedges, and your favorite sides.

Tips:

- Always use caution when handling live lobsters.
- Steam the lobsters in batches if your pot is not large enough to accommodate them all at once.
- The cooking time may vary slightly based on the size of the lobsters and the altitude of your location.
- Serve the steamed lobster with additional sides like corn on the cob, coleslaw, or potatoes for a traditional New England feast.

Steamed lobster is a simple and classic way to enjoy the natural flavors of this seafood delicacy. Whether it's a special occasion or just a delicious meal, steamed lobster is sure to be a hit.

Codfish Cakes

Ingredients:

- 1 pound cod fillets (fresh or salted and soaked to remove excess salt)
- 2 cups mashed potatoes (prepared and cooled)
- 1/2 cup finely chopped onion
- 1/4 cup chopped fresh parsley
- 2 tablespoons mayonnaise
- 1 tablespoon Dijon mustard
- 1 teaspoon Worcestershire sauce
- Salt and pepper to taste
- 1 cup breadcrumbs (for coating)
- Vegetable oil for frying

Instructions:

Prepare the Cod:
- If using salted cod, soak it in water for several hours or overnight to remove excess salt. If using fresh cod, pat it dry with paper towels. Cook the cod by poaching or baking until it's flaky. Once cooked, flake the cod into small pieces.

Mix Ingredients:
- In a large mixing bowl, combine the flaked cod, mashed potatoes, chopped onion, fresh parsley, mayonnaise, Dijon mustard, Worcestershire sauce, salt, and pepper. Mix the ingredients until well combined.

Form Codfish Cakes:
- Divide the mixture into equal portions and shape them into round or oval cakes.

Coat with Breadcrumbs:
- Roll each codfish cake in breadcrumbs, ensuring they are evenly coated on all sides.

Heat Vegetable Oil:
- In a large skillet, heat vegetable oil over medium heat. Make sure there's enough oil to shallow fry the cakes.

Fry Codfish Cakes:
- Carefully place the codfish cakes in the hot oil. Fry them until golden brown on each side, approximately 3-4 minutes per side.

Drain and Serve:
- Once the codfish cakes are cooked through and crispy on the outside, transfer them to a plate lined with paper towels to drain excess oil.

Serve Warm:
- Serve the codfish cakes warm, either as a main dish or as an appetizer. They pair well with tartar sauce, remoulade, or a squeeze of lemon.

Optional Tips:

- You can customize the flavor by adding ingredients like chopped green onions, garlic, or Old Bay seasoning.
- For an extra kick, add a pinch of cayenne pepper or hot sauce to the mixture.
- Make smaller cakes for bite-sized appetizers or larger ones for a main course.

Codfish cakes are a delicious and versatile dish that can be enjoyed on various occasions. Adjust the seasoning and accompaniments based on your preferences for a delightful culinary experience.

Boston Cream Cupcakes

Ingredients:

For the Cupcakes:

- 1 1/2 cups all-purpose flour
- 1 1/2 teaspoons baking powder
- 1/2 teaspoon salt
- 1/2 cup unsalted butter, softened
- 1 cup granulated sugar
- 2 large eggs
- 1 teaspoon vanilla extract
- 1/2 cup whole milk

For the Custard Filling:

- 1 cup whole milk
- 1/4 cup granulated sugar
- 3 large egg yolks
- 2 tablespoons cornstarch
- 1/8 teaspoon salt
- 1 teaspoon vanilla extract

For the Chocolate Ganache:

- 1/2 cup heavy cream
- 1 cup semisweet chocolate chips
- 1 tablespoon unsalted butter

Instructions:

Make the Cupcakes:

    Preheat the Oven:
- Preheat your oven to 350°F (175°C). Line a cupcake tin with paper liners.

    Mix Dry Ingredients:
- In a bowl, whisk together the flour, baking powder, and salt.

    Cream Butter and Sugar:

- In a separate large bowl, cream together the softened butter and granulated sugar until light and fluffy.

Add Eggs and Vanilla:
- Add the eggs one at a time, beating well after each addition. Stir in the vanilla extract.

Alternate Flour and Milk:
- Gradually add the dry ingredients to the wet ingredients, alternating with the milk. Begin and end with the dry ingredients, mixing until just combined.

Fill Cupcake Liners:
- Divide the batter evenly among the cupcake liners, filling each about two-thirds full.

Bake:
- Bake in the preheated oven for 18-20 minutes or until a toothpick inserted into the center of a cupcake comes out clean.

Cool:
- Allow the cupcakes to cool in the tin for a few minutes, then transfer them to a wire rack to cool completely.

Make the Custard Filling:

Heat Milk:
- In a saucepan, heat the milk until it just begins to simmer.

Whisk Yolks and Sugar:
- In a bowl, whisk together the egg yolks and sugar until well combined.

Add Cornstarch:
- Add the cornstarch to the egg yolk mixture and whisk until smooth.

Temper the Eggs:
- Slowly pour the hot milk into the egg yolk mixture, whisking constantly to temper the eggs.

Cook Custard:
- Return the mixture to the saucepan and cook over medium heat, whisking constantly, until it thickens into a custard-like consistency.

Remove from Heat:
- Remove the custard from the heat, stir in the salt and vanilla extract. Let it cool.

Fill the Cupcakes:

Create a Well:
- Once the cupcakes are cooled, use a knife to create a well in the center of each cupcake.

Fill with Custard:
- Fill each well with the cooled custard.

Make the Chocolate Ganache:

Heat Cream:
- In a saucepan, heat the heavy cream until it just begins to simmer.

Pour Over Chocolate:
- Pour the hot cream over the chocolate chips and let it sit for a minute. Stir until smooth.

Add Butter:
- Stir in the butter until it's fully melted and incorporated.

Cool Slightly:
- Let the ganache cool for a few minutes until it thickens slightly.

Top the Cupcakes:

Dip and Coat:
- Dip the top of each cupcake into the chocolate ganache, coating the custard-filled well.

Cool and Set:
- Allow the ganache to cool and set before serving.

Enjoy:
- Serve and enjoy these Boston Cream Cupcakes with the luscious combination of custard and chocolate ganache.

These Boston Cream Cupcakes are a delightful twist on the classic dessert, and they are sure to be a hit for any occasion.

Brown Bread Ice Cream

Ingredients:

For the Brown Bread Crumbs:

- 2 slices brown bread (preferably whole wheat)
- 2 tablespoons unsalted butter, melted
- 2 tablespoons brown sugar
- 1/4 teaspoon ground cinnamon

For the Ice Cream Base:

- 2 cups heavy cream
- 1 cup whole milk
- 3/4 cup granulated sugar
- 1 teaspoon vanilla extract
- Pinch of salt

Instructions:

Prepare Brown Bread Crumbs:

    Preheat Oven:
- Preheat your oven to 350°F (175°C).

    Make Crumbs:
- In a food processor, pulse the brown bread slices into coarse crumbs.

    Mix with Butter and Sugar:
- In a bowl, combine the brown bread crumbs with melted butter, brown sugar, and ground cinnamon. Toss until the crumbs are coated.

    Toast in Oven:
- Spread the coated crumbs on a baking sheet and toast in the preheated oven for about 10-12 minutes or until golden brown. Stir occasionally to ensure even toasting. Allow the crumbs to cool.

Prepare Ice Cream Base:

Mix Ingredients:
- In a mixing bowl, whisk together heavy cream, whole milk, granulated sugar, vanilla extract, and a pinch of salt until the sugar is dissolved.

Chill Mixture:
- Cover the bowl and refrigerate the mixture for at least 4 hours or overnight to chill thoroughly.

Churn Ice Cream:
- Pour the chilled mixture into an ice cream maker and churn according to the manufacturer's instructions until it reaches a soft-serve consistency.

Add Brown Bread Crumbs:
- During the last few minutes of churning, gradually add the toasted brown bread crumbs into the ice cream maker. Let the machine mix them evenly into the ice cream.

Transfer and Freeze:
- Transfer the churned ice cream into a lidded container, spreading it evenly. Freeze for at least 4 hours or until firm.

Serve and Enjoy:
- Scoop the Brown Bread Ice Cream into bowls or cones. Optionally, sprinkle extra brown bread crumbs on top for added crunch.

This Brown Bread Ice Cream offers a delightful contrast of creamy sweetness with the nutty and toasty flavor of brown bread crumbs. It's a unique and satisfying treat that will surprise and delight your taste buds.

New England Clam Dip

Ingredients:

- 1 can (6.5 ounces) minced or chopped clams, drained (reserve clam juice)
- 1 package (8 ounces) cream cheese, softened
- 1/2 cup mayonnaise
- 1 tablespoon lemon juice
- 1 teaspoon Worcestershire sauce
- 1/2 teaspoon onion powder
- 1/4 teaspoon garlic powder
- Salt and black pepper to taste
- Chopped fresh parsley for garnish (optional)
- Crackers or chips for serving

Instructions:

Prepare Clams:
- Drain the clam juice from the can of clams, reserving the juice for later use.

Softened Cream Cheese:
- In a mixing bowl, ensure the cream cheese is softened to room temperature.

Mix Ingredients:
- Add the drained clams, mayonnaise, lemon juice, Worcestershire sauce, onion powder, garlic powder, salt, and black pepper to the softened cream cheese.

Combine Thoroughly:
- Mix the ingredients thoroughly until well combined. You can use a hand mixer or mix by hand.

Adjust Consistency:
- If the dip is too thick, you can add a bit of the reserved clam juice to achieve your desired consistency. Add a little at a time and mix until it reaches the desired thickness.

Chill:
- Cover the clam dip and refrigerate for at least 1-2 hours to allow the flavors to meld and the dip to chill.

Garnish and Serve:

- Before serving, garnish the clam dip with chopped fresh parsley if desired.

Serve with Crackers or Chips:
- Serve the New England Clam Dip with your favorite crackers, tortilla chips, or vegetable sticks.

Enjoy:
- Enjoy this flavorful and creamy clam dip as an appetizer or party snack.

Optional Tips:

- For an extra kick, you can add a dash of hot sauce or a pinch of cayenne pepper.
- Adjust the seasoning to your taste preference, adding more lemon juice, Worcestershire sauce, or spices as needed.

This New England Clam Dip is a crowd-pleaser, and its creamy, savory flavors make it a perfect addition to your appetizer spread for parties, gatherings, or game nights.

Boiled Lobster Dinner

Ingredients:

- Live lobsters (1-1.5 pounds each)
- Salt

Equipment:

- Large pot with a tight-fitting lid
- Tongs or lobster crackers
- Butter and lemon wedges for serving

Instructions:

Prepare the Lobsters:
- Choose live lobsters for the freshest taste. Check for lively movement and make sure they are not lethargic. Rinse them under cold water.

Fill the Pot:
- Fill a large pot with enough water to fully submerge the lobsters. Add salt to the water, aiming for about 2-3 tablespoons of salt per gallon of water.

Boil Water:
- Bring the salted water to a rolling boil.

Insert Lobsters:
- Carefully place the live lobsters into the boiling water headfirst. Be cautious, as they may be quite active.

Cover and Boil:
- Immediately cover the pot with a tight-fitting lid. Boil the lobsters for about 10-12 minutes for the first pound, and add 3 minutes for each additional pound. For example, a 2-pound lobster would boil for about 13-15 minutes.

Check Doneness:
- The lobsters are done when they turn a bright red color, and the antennae can be easily pulled off. The internal temperature should reach 140°F (60°C).

Remove and Serve:
- Use tongs to carefully remove the lobsters from the pot. Allow them to drain for a moment.

Crack and Serve:

- Use lobster crackers or kitchen shears to crack open the lobster shells. Serve with melted butter and lemon wedges on the side.

Tips:

- Always use caution when handling live lobsters.
- Serve the boiled lobster with additional sides like corn on the cob, coleslaw, or potatoes for a traditional New England lobster dinner.
- Provide lobster bibs and plenty of napkins, as cracking open lobster shells can be messy.

Boiling lobster is a simple and delicious way to enjoy this seafood delicacy. Whether you're hosting a special occasion or just treating yourself, a boiled lobster dinner is a classic and flavorful choice.

Boston Baked Scrod

Ingredients:

- 1 1/2 pounds scrod fillets (or other white fish like cod or haddock)
- 1/2 cup breadcrumbs (fresh or seasoned)
- 2 tablespoons melted butter
- 2 tablespoons fresh parsley, chopped
- 1 clove garlic, minced
- 1 teaspoon Dijon mustard
- 1 teaspoon lemon juice
- Salt and pepper to taste
- Lemon wedges for serving

Instructions:

Preheat Oven:
- Preheat your oven to 375°F (190°C).

Prepare Baking Dish:
- Lightly grease a baking dish that's large enough to accommodate the scrod fillets in a single layer.

Prepare Crumb Topping:
- In a bowl, combine the breadcrumbs, melted butter, chopped parsley, minced garlic, Dijon mustard, lemon juice, salt, and pepper. Mix well until the breadcrumbs are evenly coated.

Coat Scrod:
- Place the scrod fillets in the prepared baking dish. Pat them dry with a paper towel. Season the fillets with a little salt and pepper.

Top with Crumb Mixture:
- Evenly distribute the crumb topping over the scrod fillets, pressing it down slightly to adhere.

Bake:
- Bake in the preheated oven for about 15-20 minutes or until the fish is opaque and flakes easily with a fork. The crumb topping should be golden brown and crispy.

Serve:
- Remove the Boston Baked Scrod from the oven and serve hot. Squeeze fresh lemon juice over the top before serving.

Garnish:

- Garnish with additional chopped parsley if desired.

Tips:

- Adjust the seasoning of the crumb mixture to your taste. You can add a pinch of paprika or a dash of cayenne for extra flavor.
- Serve Boston Baked Scrod with sides like mashed potatoes, steamed vegetables, or a green salad.

This Boston Baked Scrod recipe is a simple yet flavorful way to enjoy white fish with a delightful crispy topping. It's a classic New England dish that makes for a satisfying and delicious meal.

Apple Cider Glazed Pork Chops

Ingredients:

- 4 bone-in pork chops
- Salt and black pepper to taste
- 2 tablespoons olive oil

For the Apple Cider Glaze:

- 1 cup apple cider
- 2 tablespoons Dijon mustard
- 2 tablespoons maple syrup
- 1 tablespoon apple cider vinegar
- 1 teaspoon cornstarch (optional, for thickening)

Instructions:

Preheat Oven:
- Preheat your oven to 375°F (190°C).

Season Pork Chops:
- Season the pork chops with salt and black pepper on both sides.

Sear Pork Chops:
- In an oven-safe skillet, heat the olive oil over medium-high heat. Sear the pork chops for about 2-3 minutes on each side, or until they develop a golden-brown crust.

Prepare Apple Cider Glaze:
- In a small bowl, whisk together the apple cider, Dijon mustard, maple syrup, and apple cider vinegar to create the glaze.

Add Glaze to Skillet:
- Pour the apple cider glaze over the seared pork chops in the skillet.

Bake:
- Transfer the skillet to the preheated oven. Bake for about 15-20 minutes or until the pork chops reach an internal temperature of 145°F (63°C).

Baste with Glaze:
- Baste the pork chops with the apple cider glaze from the skillet a couple of times during the baking process.

Optional Thickening:

- If you prefer a thicker glaze, you can mix a teaspoon of cornstarch with a little water and stir it into the glaze during the last few minutes of baking. This will help thicken the sauce.

Rest and Serve:
- Remove the skillet from the oven and let the pork chops rest for a few minutes. This allows the juices to redistribute.

Serve:
- Spoon some of the apple cider glaze over the pork chops and serve them hot.

Garnish (Optional):
- Garnish with chopped fresh herbs, such as parsley or thyme, for added flavor.

Tips:

- You can marinate the pork chops in the apple cider glaze for a few hours before cooking for enhanced flavor.
- Serve the pork chops with sides like roasted vegetables, mashed potatoes, or a green salad.

These Apple Cider Glazed Pork Chops are a perfect combination of sweet and savory, making them a comforting and delicious meal. The apple cider glaze adds a delightful touch of fall flavor to the dish.

Moxie Soda Pulled Pork

Ingredients:

- 3-4 pounds pork shoulder or pork butt
- Salt and black pepper to taste
- 1 tablespoon olive oil
- 1 large onion, thinly sliced
- 3 cloves garlic, minced
- 1 can (12 ounces) Moxie soda
- 1 cup barbecue sauce
- 1/4 cup apple cider vinegar
- 1 teaspoon Dijon mustard
- 1 teaspoon Worcestershire sauce
- 1/2 teaspoon smoked paprika
- Hamburger buns, for serving

Instructions:

Preheat Oven:
- Preheat your oven to 325°F (163°C).

Season Pork:
- Season the pork shoulder or pork butt with salt and black pepper on all sides.

Sear Pork:
- In a large oven-safe Dutch oven or skillet, heat olive oil over medium-high heat. Sear the pork on all sides until browned. Remove the pork from the pot and set it aside.

Sauté Onion and Garlic:
- In the same pot, add sliced onions and minced garlic. Sauté until the onions are softened and translucent.

Prepare Moxie Soda Sauce:
- In a bowl, mix together the Moxie soda, barbecue sauce, apple cider vinegar, Dijon mustard, Worcestershire sauce, and smoked paprika.

Braise Pork:
- Place the seared pork back into the pot with the onions and garlic. Pour the Moxie soda sauce over the pork.

Cover and Bake:

- Cover the pot with a lid or aluminum foil. Transfer it to the preheated oven and bake for approximately 3-4 hours or until the pork is tender and easily shreds with a fork.

Shred Pork:
- Remove the pork from the pot and use two forks to shred it into bite-sized pieces. Discard any excess fat.

Reduce Sauce:
- If the sauce is too thin, you can transfer it to a separate pot and simmer over medium heat to reduce and thicken it.

Combine Shredded Pork and Sauce:
- Mix the shredded pork with the reduced sauce, ensuring it's well coated.

Serve:
- Serve the Moxie Soda Pulled Pork on hamburger buns. You can add coleslaw or pickles as toppings if desired.

Enjoy:
- Enjoy this unique and flavorful Moxie Soda Pulled Pork with the distinctive taste of Moxie soda.

Tips:

- If you can't find Moxie soda, you can try substituting with another soda, but keep in mind that it will alter the flavor profile of the dish.
- Adjust the barbecue sauce quantity based on your taste preferences. If you like it saucier, add more; if you prefer less sauce, reduce the amount.

Moxie Soda Pulled Pork is a creative and tasty twist on traditional pulled pork, offering a unique flavor experience with the addition of Moxie soda.

New England Apple Cake

Ingredients:

- 2 cups all-purpose flour
- 1 teaspoon baking soda
- 1/2 teaspoon baking powder
- 1/2 teaspoon salt
- 1 teaspoon ground cinnamon
- 1/2 teaspoon ground nutmeg
- 1/2 cup unsalted butter, softened
- 1 cup granulated sugar
- 2 large eggs
- 1 teaspoon vanilla extract
- 1/2 cup sour cream
- 2 cups peeled and chopped apples (such as Granny Smith or Honeycrisp)
- 1 cup chopped nuts (walnuts or pecans), optional

For the Glaze:

- 1 cup confectioners' sugar
- 2 tablespoons milk
- 1/2 teaspoon vanilla extract

Instructions:

Preheat Oven:
- Preheat your oven to 350°F (175°C). Grease and flour a 9x13-inch baking pan.

Prepare Dry Ingredients:
- In a medium bowl, whisk together the flour, baking soda, baking powder, salt, cinnamon, and nutmeg. Set aside.

Cream Butter and Sugar:
- In a large bowl, cream together the softened butter and granulated sugar until light and fluffy.

Add Eggs and Vanilla:
- Add the eggs one at a time, beating well after each addition. Stir in the vanilla extract.

Alternate Flour and Sour Cream:

- Gradually add the dry ingredients to the wet ingredients, alternating with the sour cream. Begin and end with the dry ingredients, mixing until just combined.

Fold in Apples and Nuts:
- Gently fold in the chopped apples and nuts (if using) until evenly distributed throughout the batter.

Transfer to Baking Pan:
- Spread the batter evenly into the prepared 9x13-inch baking pan.

Bake:
- Bake in the preheated oven for 40-45 minutes or until a toothpick inserted into the center comes out clean and the top is golden brown.

Make Glaze:
- While the cake is baking, prepare the glaze. In a small bowl, whisk together the confectioners' sugar, milk, and vanilla extract until smooth.

Cool Cake:
- Allow the cake to cool in the pan for about 10 minutes.

Drizzle Glaze:
- Drizzle the glaze over the warm cake. Allow the cake to cool completely before cutting into squares.

Serve and Enjoy:
- Serve the New England Apple Cake squares on their own or with a dollop of whipped cream or a scoop of vanilla ice cream.

Optional Tips:

- You can add a sprinkle of powdered sugar or a dash of cinnamon on top for extra garnish.
- Experiment with different apple varieties to find your preferred flavor and texture.

This New England Apple Cake is a wonderful way to celebrate the fall season with the sweet and spiced goodness of apples. It's perfect for gatherings, dessert tables, or simply enjoying a cozy evening treat.

Boston Brown Bread Muffins

Ingredients:

- 1 cup whole wheat flour
- 1/2 cup cornmeal
- 1/2 cup all-purpose flour
- 1 teaspoon baking soda
- 1/2 teaspoon salt
- 3/4 cup buttermilk
- 1/3 cup molasses
- 1/4 cup unsalted butter, melted
- 1/3 cup raisins (optional)

Instructions:

Preheat Oven:
- Preheat your oven to 375°F (190°C). Grease a muffin tin or line it with paper liners.

Mix Dry Ingredients:
- In a large bowl, whisk together the whole wheat flour, cornmeal, all-purpose flour, baking soda, and salt.

Combine Wet Ingredients:
- In a separate bowl, mix together the buttermilk, molasses, and melted butter.

Combine Wet and Dry Mixtures:
- Pour the wet ingredients into the dry ingredients and stir until just combined. Do not overmix. If using raisins, gently fold them into the batter.

Fill Muffin Cups:
- Divide the batter evenly among the muffin cups, filling each about 2/3 full.

Bake:
- Bake in the preheated oven for 15-18 minutes or until a toothpick inserted into the center of a muffin comes out clean.

Cool:
- Allow the muffins to cool in the tin for a few minutes, then transfer them to a wire rack to cool completely.

Serve and Enjoy:

- Serve the Boston Brown Bread Muffins warm or at room temperature. They are delicious on their own or with a spread of butter.

Optional Tips:

- You can add other mix-ins like chopped nuts or dried fruit for added texture and flavor.
- Serve these muffins as a side with Boston baked beans, a classic pairing in New England cuisine.

These Boston Brown Bread Muffins offer a convenient and portable way to enjoy the rich flavors of traditional Boston brown bread. They are perfect for breakfast, brunch, or as a side dish with savory meals.

Maple Walnut Fudge

Ingredients:

- 3 cups granulated sugar
- 3/4 cup unsalted butter
- 2/3 cup evaporated milk
- 1 cup real maple syrup
- 1 teaspoon vanilla extract
- 2 cups marshmallow cream
- 1 1/2 cups chopped walnuts, toasted

Instructions:

Prepare Pan:
- Line a 9x9-inch square baking pan with parchment paper, leaving some overhang for easy removal. Grease the parchment paper with butter.

Toast Walnuts:
- In a dry skillet over medium heat, toast the chopped walnuts until they become fragrant and lightly browned. Stir frequently to avoid burning. Remove from heat and set aside.

Combine Ingredients:
- In a large, heavy-bottomed saucepan, combine sugar, butter, evaporated milk, and maple syrup. Cook over medium heat, stirring constantly until the mixture comes to a boil.

Boil:
- Once boiling, continue to stir and cook until a candy thermometer reads 234°F (112°C) or until the soft ball stage is reached. This may take around 5-7 minutes.

Remove from Heat:
- Remove the saucepan from heat and quickly stir in the vanilla extract, marshmallow cream, and toasted walnuts. Mix until well combined.

Pour into Pan:
- Immediately pour the hot mixture into the prepared baking pan, spreading it evenly with a spatula.

Cool:
- Allow the Maple Walnut Fudge to cool at room temperature until it sets, which may take a few hours.

Chill (Optional):
- For faster setting, you can refrigerate the fudge for a couple of hours.

Cut into Squares:
- Once the fudge has completely set, use the parchment paper overhang to lift it out of the pan. Place it on a cutting board and cut it into squares.

Serve and Enjoy:
- Serve the Maple Walnut Fudge squares and enjoy the delicious combination of maple sweetness and crunchy walnuts.

Optional Tips:

- Make sure to use real maple syrup for the authentic maple flavor.
- If you don't have a candy thermometer, you can perform the soft ball test by dropping a small amount of the mixture into a cup of cold water. If it forms a soft ball, it's ready.
- Experiment with different nuts or add a sprinkle of sea salt on top for additional flavor.

This Maple Walnut Fudge is a wonderful homemade treat that captures the essence of maple and the crunch of toasted walnuts. It's perfect for holiday gatherings, gifts, or satisfying your sweet tooth any time of the year.

New England Fried Clams

Ingredients:

- 2 pounds whole belly clams, shucked
- 1 cup all-purpose flour
- 1 cup cornmeal
- 1 teaspoon baking powder
- 1 teaspoon salt
- 1/2 teaspoon black pepper
- 1/2 teaspoon paprika
- 1 cup buttermilk
- Vegetable oil for frying
- Lemon wedges for serving
- Tartar sauce or cocktail sauce for dipping

Instructions:

Prepare Clams:
- Make sure the clam bellies are clean and free of excess sand. If they are large, you can cut them into bite-sized pieces.

Prepare Batter:
- In a bowl, whisk together the flour, cornmeal, baking powder, salt, black pepper, and paprika.

Dip Clams in Buttermilk:
- Dip the cleaned clam bellies into the buttermilk, ensuring they are well-coated.

Coat with Batter:
- Take the clams from the buttermilk and dredge them in the seasoned flour-cornmeal mixture, pressing the coating onto the clams to adhere.

Heat Oil:
- In a deep fryer or a heavy-bottomed pot, heat enough vegetable oil to reach a temperature of 350°F (175°C).

Fry in Batches:
- Carefully lower the coated clams into the hot oil in batches, ensuring they are not overcrowded. Fry for 2-3 minutes or until golden brown and crispy.

Drain and Repeat:

- Use a slotted spoon to remove the fried clams from the oil and place them on a plate lined with paper towels to drain excess oil. Repeat the process with the remaining clams.

Serve Hot:
- Serve the New England Fried Clams hot with lemon wedges and your choice of tartar sauce or cocktail sauce for dipping.

Enjoy:
- Enjoy the crispy, golden-brown goodness of New England Fried Clams as a delicious appetizer or main course.

Optional Tips:

- If whole belly clams are not available, you can use clam strips, but the whole bellies provide a more authentic experience.
- Adjust the seasoning in the batter to your liking, adding more or less paprika, black pepper, or salt.
- Serve the fried clams with a side of coleslaw or french fries for a classic seafood platter.

This recipe brings the flavors of New England seafood shacks to your kitchen, allowing you to savor the crispy and succulent goodness of fried clams at home.

Cranberry Walnut Bread

Ingredients:

- 2 cups all-purpose flour
- 1 cup granulated sugar
- 1 1/2 teaspoons baking powder
- 1/2 teaspoon baking soda
- 1/2 teaspoon salt
- 1 cup fresh or frozen cranberries, coarsely chopped
- 1/2 cup chopped walnuts
- 1 large egg
- 1 cup buttermilk
- 1/4 cup unsalted butter, melted
- 1 teaspoon vanilla extract
- Zest of one orange (optional)

Instructions:

Preheat Oven:
- Preheat your oven to 350°F (175°C). Grease and flour a 9x5-inch loaf pan.

Mix Dry Ingredients:
- In a large bowl, whisk together the flour, sugar, baking powder, baking soda, and salt.

Add Cranberries and Walnuts:
- Gently fold in the chopped cranberries and walnuts until evenly distributed throughout the dry ingredients.

Whisk Wet Ingredients:
- In a separate bowl, whisk together the egg, buttermilk, melted butter, vanilla extract, and orange zest if using.

Combine Wet and Dry Mixtures:
- Pour the wet ingredients into the dry ingredients. Stir until just combined, being careful not to overmix. The batter will be thick.

Transfer to Pan:
- Transfer the batter into the prepared loaf pan, spreading it evenly.

Bake:
- Bake in the preheated oven for 55-60 minutes or until a toothpick inserted into the center comes out clean or with a few moist crumbs.

Cool:
- Allow the Cranberry Walnut Bread to cool in the pan for about 10 minutes before transferring it to a wire rack to cool completely.

Slice and Serve:
- Once completely cooled, slice the bread and serve. It's delicious on its own or with a smear of butter.

Optional Tips:

- You can use dried cranberries if fresh or frozen ones are not available. If using dried cranberries, you might want to soak them in hot water for 10-15 minutes and then drain before adding to the batter.
- Substitute orange juice for the buttermilk for an extra citrusy flavor.
- If you prefer a sweeter bread, you can increase the sugar to 1 1/2 cups.

This Cranberry Walnut Bread is perfect for breakfast, brunch, or as a delightful snack.

The combination of tart cranberries and crunchy walnuts makes it a festive treat,

especially during the holiday season.

Rhode Island Johnnycakes

Ingredients:

- 1 cup cornmeal
- 1/2 teaspoon salt
- 1 1/4 cups boiling water
- Butter or oil for cooking

Instructions:

Mix Cornmeal and Salt:
- In a mixing bowl, combine the cornmeal and salt.

Add Boiling Water:
- Pour the boiling water over the cornmeal mixture. Stir well to create a thick batter. Let the batter rest for a few minutes to allow the cornmeal to absorb the water.

Form Pancakes:
- Heat a griddle or non-stick skillet over medium heat. Add a small amount of butter or oil to coat the surface.

Drop Batter on Griddle:
- Spoon the batter onto the hot griddle to form pancakes. You can make them any size you prefer.

Cook Until Golden Brown:
- Cook the Johnny Cakes until the edges are crisp and golden brown, about 3-5 minutes per side.

Serve Hot:
- Serve the Rhode Island Johnnycakes hot with your favorite toppings. Traditional toppings include butter, maple syrup, honey, or even savory options like cheese or bacon.

Optional Tips:

- Adjust the thickness of the batter based on your preference. Thicker batter will result in heartier cakes, while thinner batter will produce lighter ones.
- Experiment with the ratio of cornmeal to water to achieve the texture you desire.
- If you prefer a sweeter version, you can add a touch of sugar to the batter or serve the Johnnycakes with sweet toppings like fruit preserves.

Rhode Island Johnnycakes are a versatile dish that can be enjoyed for breakfast, brunch, or as a side dish with savory meals. They have a unique texture and flavor that make them a beloved part of New England culinary traditions.

Baked Stuffed Lobster

Ingredients:

- 2 live lobsters (about 1.5 to 2 pounds each)
- 1 cup fresh breadcrumbs
- 1/4 cup unsalted butter, melted
- 2 tablespoons fresh parsley, chopped
- 2 tablespoons fresh chives, chopped
- 1 clove garlic, minced
- 1/4 cup grated Parmesan cheese
- Salt and black pepper to taste
- Lemon wedges for serving
- Additional melted butter for drizzling

Instructions:

Preheat Oven:
- Preheat your oven to 375°F (190°C).

Prepare Lobsters:
- If the lobsters are live, quickly and humanely dispatch them by placing them in the freezer for about 30 minutes before cooking. Cut the lobsters in half lengthwise, splitting the body and tail into two halves.

Remove Meat from Shell:
- Remove the lobster meat from the tail and claws, keeping it in one piece if possible. Chop the lobster meat into bite-sized chunks.

Prepare Stuffing:
- In a bowl, combine the fresh breadcrumbs, melted butter, chopped parsley, chopped chives, minced garlic, grated Parmesan cheese, salt, and black pepper. Mix well to create the stuffing mixture.

Stuff Lobster Shells:
- Place the lobster halves in a baking dish, cut side up. Distribute the stuffing mixture evenly among the lobster shells, pressing it down gently.

Bake:
- Bake in the preheated oven for about 20-25 minutes or until the lobster meat is cooked through, and the stuffing is golden brown.

Serve:
- Remove the Baked Stuffed Lobster from the oven. Drizzle with additional melted butter and serve hot with lemon wedges on the side.

Enjoy:
- Enjoy the indulgent and flavorful Baked Stuffed Lobster as a main course for a special occasion or celebration.

Optional Tips:

- Customize the stuffing by adding ingredients like chopped crabmeat, shrimp, or additional herbs for extra flavor.
- If you prefer a crispier topping, you can place the stuffed lobsters under the broiler for a minute or two at the end of the baking time.

Baked Stuffed Lobster is a luxurious and impressive dish that's perfect for showcasing the rich, sweet flavor of lobster. It's sure to be a hit at any special dinner or celebration.

Anadama Bread

Ingredients:

- 1 cup yellow cornmeal
- 1 cup boiling water
- 1/2 cup molasses
- 1/4 cup unsalted butter
- 1 teaspoon salt
- 1/2 cup warm water (about 110°F or 43°C)
- 1 package (2 1/4 teaspoons) active dry yeast
- 3 1/2 to 4 cups all-purpose flour

Instructions:

Prepare Cornmeal Mixture:
- In a heatproof bowl, combine the cornmeal and boiling water. Stir well and let it sit for about 10 minutes to allow the cornmeal to absorb the water.

Add Molasses and Butter:
- Add molasses, butter, and salt to the cornmeal mixture. Stir until the butter is melted, and the mixture is well combined. Allow it to cool to lukewarm.

Activate Yeast:
- In a small bowl, dissolve the yeast in warm water. Let it sit for 5-10 minutes until it becomes frothy.

Combine Mixtures:
- In a large mixing bowl, combine the cornmeal mixture with the activated yeast. Stir to mix.

Add Flour:
- Gradually add the flour, one cup at a time, stirring well after each addition. Continue adding flour until the dough comes together and can be kneaded.

Knead Dough:
- Turn the dough onto a floured surface and knead for about 8-10 minutes until it becomes smooth and elastic. Add more flour as needed to prevent sticking.

First Rise:
- Place the dough in a greased bowl, cover it with a clean kitchen towel, and let it rise in a warm place for about 1 to 1.5 hours, or until it has doubled in size.

Shape and Second Rise:
- Punch down the dough and shape it into a loaf. Place the shaped dough in a greased bread pan. Cover it again and let it rise for another 45-60 minutes.

Preheat Oven:
- Preheat your oven to 375°F (190°C).

Bake:
- Bake the Anadama Bread in the preheated oven for 30-35 minutes or until the top is golden brown and the loaf sounds hollow when tapped on the bottom.

Cool:
- Allow the bread to cool in the pan for 10 minutes before transferring it to a wire rack to cool completely.

Slice and Enjoy:
- Slice the Anadama Bread and enjoy it as is or toasted with butter.

Optional Tips:

- You can add a tablespoon of sesame seeds or sunflower seeds to the dough for added texture and flavor.
- Some variations include incorporating a small amount of grated orange zest or ground cinnamon for extra depth.

Anadama Bread is a unique and flavorful bread that can be enjoyed on its own or as part of a sandwich. Its slightly sweet and hearty profile makes it a favorite in New England cuisine.

Boston Cream Pie Cupcake

Ingredients:

For the Cupcakes:

- 1 1/2 cups all-purpose flour
- 1 1/2 teaspoons baking powder
- 1/2 teaspoon salt
- 1/2 cup unsalted butter, softened
- 1 cup granulated sugar
- 2 large eggs
- 1 teaspoon vanilla extract
- 1/2 cup whole milk

For the Custard Filling:

- 1 cup whole milk
- 3 large egg yolks
- 1/3 cup granulated sugar
- 2 tablespoons cornstarch
- 1/4 teaspoon salt
- 1 teaspoon vanilla extract

For the Chocolate Ganache:

- 1/2 cup heavy cream
- 1/2 cup semisweet chocolate chips
- 1 tablespoon unsalted butter

Instructions:

For the Cupcakes:

Preheat Oven:
- Preheat your oven to 350°F (175°C). Line a cupcake tin with paper liners.

Mix Dry Ingredients:

- In a bowl, whisk together the flour, baking powder, and salt. Set aside.

Cream Butter and Sugar:
- In a separate large bowl, cream together the softened butter and granulated sugar until light and fluffy.

Add Eggs and Vanilla:
- Add the eggs one at a time, beating well after each addition. Stir in the vanilla extract.

Alternate Dry Ingredients and Milk:
- Gradually add the dry ingredients to the wet ingredients, alternating with the milk. Begin and end with the dry ingredients. Mix until just combined.

Fill Cupcake Liners:
- Divide the batter evenly among the cupcake liners, filling each about 2/3 full.

Bake:
- Bake in the preheated oven for 18-20 minutes or until a toothpick inserted into the center of a cupcake comes out clean. Allow the cupcakes to cool completely.

For the Custard Filling:

Heat Milk:
- In a saucepan, heat the milk until it just begins to simmer.

Whisk Egg Yolks and Sugar:
- In a separate bowl, whisk together the egg yolks, sugar, cornstarch, and salt until well combined.

Temper Eggs:
- Gradually whisk the hot milk into the egg yolk mixture to temper the eggs.

Cook Custard:
- Return the mixture to the saucepan and cook over medium heat, stirring constantly, until the custard thickens. Remove from heat and stir in the vanilla extract.

Cool Custard:
- Allow the custard to cool completely. You can place plastic wrap directly on the surface to prevent a skin from forming.

For the Chocolate Ganache:

Heat Cream:

- In a small saucepan, heat the heavy cream until it just starts to simmer.

Pour Over Chocolate:
- Pour the hot cream over the chocolate chips in a heatproof bowl. Let it sit for a minute, then stir until smooth. Add the butter and stir until melted and well combined.

Assembly:

Core Cupcakes:
- Use a cupcake corer or a small knife to remove the center of each cupcake.

Fill with Custard:
- Fill each cored cupcake with the cooled custard.

Top with Ganache:
- Spoon or dip the top of each cupcake into the chocolate ganache, allowing it to set slightly.

Chill (Optional):
- If desired, you can refrigerate the cupcakes briefly to help the ganache set.

Serve and Enjoy:
- Serve the Boston Cream Pie Cupcakes and enjoy the individual-sized portions of this classic treat.

Optional Tips:

- If you don't have a cupcake corer, you can use a small spoon or knife to create a well in the center of each cupcake.
- Add a touch of extra sweetness by sprinkling chocolate shavings or grated chocolate on top of the ganache.
- These cupcakes are best enjoyed on the day they are assembled for optimal freshness.

Boston Cream Pie Cupcakes offer all the deliciousness of the classic dessert in a convenient and portable form. They make a perfect treat for special occasions or anytime you're craving a delightful combination of vanilla, custard, and chocolate.

Cranberry Orange Muffins

Ingredients:

- 2 cups all-purpose flour
- 1 cup granulated sugar
- 1 1/2 teaspoons baking powder
- 1/2 teaspoon baking soda
- 1/4 teaspoon salt
- 1 cup fresh or frozen cranberries, coarsely chopped
- Zest of 1 orange
- 1/2 cup unsalted butter, melted
- 2/3 cup freshly squeezed orange juice
- 2 large eggs
- 1 teaspoon vanilla extract

For the Glaze:

- 1 cup confectioners' sugar
- 2 tablespoons freshly squeezed orange juice

Instructions:

Preheat Oven:
- Preheat your oven to 375°F (190°C). Line a muffin tin with paper liners.

Mix Dry Ingredients:
- In a large bowl, whisk together the flour, sugar, baking powder, baking soda, and salt.

Add Cranberries and Orange Zest:
- Gently fold in the chopped cranberries and orange zest into the dry ingredients.

Mix Wet Ingredients:
- In a separate bowl, mix together the melted butter, orange juice, eggs, and vanilla extract.

Combine Wet and Dry Mixtures:
- Pour the wet ingredients into the dry ingredients. Stir until just combined. Do not overmix; it's okay if there are a few lumps.

Fill Muffin Cups:
- Divide the batter evenly among the muffin cups, filling each about 2/3 full.

Bake:
- Bake in the preheated oven for 18-20 minutes or until a toothpick inserted into the center of a muffin comes out clean or with a few moist crumbs.

Make Glaze:
- While the muffins are baking, prepare the glaze. In a bowl, whisk together the confectioners' sugar and orange juice until smooth.

Cool Muffins:
- Allow the muffins to cool in the tin for a few minutes, then transfer them to a wire rack to cool completely.

Drizzle Glaze:
- Once the muffins are completely cooled, drizzle the glaze over the top of each muffin.

Serve and Enjoy:
- Serve the Cranberry Orange Muffins and enjoy the delightful combination of tart cranberries and citrus flavor.

Optional Tips:

- You can use dried cranberries if fresh or frozen ones are not available. If using dried cranberries, you might want to soak them in hot water for 10-15 minutes and then drain before adding to the batter.
- Add a touch of extra sweetness by sprinkling coarse sugar on top of the muffins before baking.
- For an extra burst of citrus flavor, you can add a tablespoon of orange zest to the glaze.

These Cranberry Orange Muffins make a perfect breakfast or snack option, combining the seasonal flavors of cranberries and the brightness of oranges. They are great for holiday gatherings or any time you want a delicious, homemade treat.

Maple Glazed Butternut Squash

Ingredients:

- 1 medium-sized butternut squash, peeled, seeded, and cut into cubes
- 2 tablespoons olive oil
- Salt and black pepper to taste
- 1/4 cup pure maple syrup
- 1 tablespoon unsalted butter (optional)
- Fresh thyme leaves for garnish (optional)

Instructions:

Preheat Oven:
- Preheat your oven to 400°F (200°C).

Prepare Butternut Squash:
- Peel the butternut squash, remove the seeds, and cut it into evenly sized cubes.

Toss with Olive Oil:
- In a large bowl, toss the butternut squash cubes with olive oil until they are well coated. Season with salt and black pepper to taste.

Roast Squash:
- Spread the seasoned butternut squash cubes in a single layer on a baking sheet. Roast in the preheated oven for 25-30 minutes or until the squash is tender and golden, stirring halfway through the cooking time for even roasting.

Prepare Maple Glaze:
- While the squash is roasting, heat the maple syrup in a small saucepan over low heat. If desired, add a tablespoon of butter to the maple syrup for extra richness. Stir until the butter is melted and the mixture is well combined.

Glaze Squash:
- Once the butternut squash is roasted, remove it from the oven. Drizzle the maple syrup glaze over the roasted squash and gently toss to coat evenly.

Return to Oven:
- Return the glazed squash to the oven and roast for an additional 5-7 minutes or until the glaze caramelizes slightly.

Garnish (Optional):

- If desired, garnish the Maple Glazed Butternut Squash with fresh thyme leaves for a burst of herbal flavor.

Serve:
- Transfer the Maple Glazed Butternut Squash to a serving dish and serve hot.

Optional Tips:

- Feel free to customize the seasoning by adding a pinch of ground cinnamon or nutmeg for a warm, spiced flavor.
- Pecans or walnuts can be added for additional crunch and nuttiness. Simply toss them with the squash during the roasting process.
- This dish pairs well with a sprinkle of crumbled feta or goat cheese for a savory contrast.

Maple Glazed Butternut Squash makes for a tasty and visually appealing side dish, perfect for fall and winter meals. The natural sweetness of the maple syrup complements the earthy flavors of the butternut squash, creating a delightful combination on your plate.

New England Seafood Bake

Ingredients:

- 1 pound large shrimp, peeled and deveined
- 1 pound mussels, cleaned and debearded
- 1 pound littleneck clams, scrubbed
- 1 pound small red potatoes, halved or quartered
- 2 ears of corn, shucked and cut into halves or thirds
- 1 pound smoked sausage (such as kielbasa), sliced
- 1 onion, thinly sliced
- 4 cloves garlic, minced
- 1/4 cup fresh parsley, chopped
- 1 lemon, sliced
- 1/2 cup unsalted butter, melted
- 1/4 cup olive oil
- 2 teaspoons Old Bay seasoning (or to taste)
- Salt and black pepper to taste
- Red pepper flakes (optional)
- Lemon wedges for serving

Instructions:

Preheat Oven:
- Preheat your oven to 425°F (220°C).

Prepare Baking Dish:
- In a large baking dish or roasting pan, combine the halved potatoes, corn pieces, sliced sausage, sliced onion, and minced garlic.

Prepare Seafood:
- In a bowl, toss the shrimp with 1 tablespoon of olive oil and a sprinkle of Old Bay seasoning. Set aside.

Arrange Ingredients:
- Arrange the clams, mussels, and seasoned shrimp on top of the vegetables in the baking dish. Sprinkle everything with chopped parsley.

Season:
- In a small bowl, mix melted butter, remaining olive oil, Old Bay seasoning, salt, black pepper, and red pepper flakes (if using). Drizzle this mixture evenly over the seafood and vegetables.

Add Lemon Slices:

- Place lemon slices on top of the seafood and vegetables.

Cover and Bake:
- Cover the baking dish tightly with aluminum foil and bake in the preheated oven for 20-25 minutes, or until the potatoes are tender and the seafood is cooked through.

Serve:
- Remove from the oven and carefully uncover. Serve the New England Seafood Bake hot, with additional lemon wedges on the side.

Optional Tips:

- Customize the seafood selection based on your preferences. You can also include other favorites like lobster tails, scallops, or crab legs.
- For an extra kick of flavor, add a splash of white wine or beer to the butter and seasoning mixture.
- Feel free to include additional vegetables such as cherry tomatoes or bell peppers for added color and flavor.

This New England Seafood Bake is a fantastic way to enjoy a variety of fresh seafood and seasonal ingredients. It's perfect for gatherings, special occasions, or simply when you're craving a flavorful and satisfying seafood feast.

Corn and Bacon Chowder

Ingredients:

- 6 slices bacon, chopped
- 1 medium onion, finely chopped
- 2 celery stalks, diced
- 2 carrots, diced
- 3 cloves garlic, minced
- 1/4 cup all-purpose flour
- 4 cups fresh or frozen corn kernels
- 4 cups chicken or vegetable broth
- 1 large potato, peeled and diced
- 1 teaspoon dried thyme
- 1 bay leaf
- 2 cups milk (whole or 2%)
- Salt and black pepper to taste
- Chopped fresh parsley for garnish (optional)

Instructions:

Cook Bacon:
- In a large pot or Dutch oven, cook the chopped bacon over medium heat until it becomes crisp. Remove some of the bacon bits for garnish and leave the rest in the pot.

Sauté Vegetables:
- Add chopped onion, diced celery, diced carrots, and minced garlic to the pot with the bacon. Sauté until the vegetables are softened, about 5-7 minutes.

Add Flour:
- Sprinkle the flour over the sautéed vegetables and bacon. Stir well to coat the vegetables, creating a roux.

Add Corn:
- Add the corn kernels to the pot and stir to combine.

Pour in Broth:
- Pour in the chicken or vegetable broth, stirring constantly to avoid lumps. Bring the mixture to a simmer.

Add Potato and Seasonings:

- Add the diced potato, dried thyme, and bay leaf to the pot. Season with salt and black pepper to taste. Simmer until the potatoes are tender, about 15-20 minutes.

Add Milk:
- Pour in the milk and continue to simmer for an additional 10-15 minutes. Adjust the seasoning if needed.

Remove Bay Leaf:
- Discard the bay leaf from the chowder.

Blend (Optional):
- For a creamier texture, you can use an immersion blender to partially blend the soup. This step is optional, and you can decide on the desired consistency.

Serve:
- Ladle the Corn and Bacon Chowder into bowls. Garnish with the reserved bacon bits and chopped fresh parsley if desired.

Enjoy:
- Serve the Corn and Bacon Chowder hot and enjoy the comforting flavors of this delicious soup.

Optional Tips:

- Add a pinch of cayenne pepper or smoked paprika for a subtle kick of heat.
- Incorporate shredded cheddar cheese for extra richness and flavor.
- If you prefer a thicker chowder, you can add more flour to the roux or use heavy cream instead of milk.

This Corn and Bacon Chowder is a wonderful way to enjoy the sweetness of corn along with the savory goodness of bacon. It's a perfect comforting soup for chilly days or anytime you're in the mood for a hearty bowl of deliciousness.

Pumpkin Whoopie Pies

Ingredients:

For the Pumpkin Cookies:

- 2 cups all-purpose flour
- 1 teaspoon baking powder
- 1/2 teaspoon baking soda
- 1/2 teaspoon salt
- 1 teaspoon ground cinnamon
- 1/2 teaspoon ground ginger
- 1/4 teaspoon ground nutmeg
- 1/2 cup unsalted butter, softened
- 1 cup granulated sugar
- 1 cup canned pumpkin puree
- 1 large egg
- 1 teaspoon vanilla extract

For the Cream Cheese Filling:

- 8 oz cream cheese, softened
- 1/2 cup unsalted butter, softened
- 2 cups confectioners' sugar
- 1 teaspoon vanilla extract

Instructions:

For the Pumpkin Cookies:

   Preheat Oven:
   - Preheat your oven to 350°F (175°C). Line baking sheets with parchment paper.

   Mix Dry Ingredients:
   - In a medium bowl, whisk together the flour, baking powder, baking soda, salt, cinnamon, ginger, and nutmeg. Set aside.

   Cream Butter and Sugar:
   - In a large bowl, cream together the softened butter and granulated sugar until light and fluffy.

   Add Pumpkin and Egg:

- Add the pumpkin puree, egg, and vanilla extract to the creamed mixture. Mix until well combined.

Add Dry Ingredients:
- Gradually add the dry ingredients to the wet ingredients, mixing until just combined. Do not overmix.

Drop Batter on Baking Sheets:
- Drop rounded tablespoons of batter onto the prepared baking sheets, spacing them about 2 inches apart.

Bake:
- Bake in the preheated oven for 10-12 minutes or until the edges are set. Allow the cookies to cool on the baking sheets for a few minutes before transferring them to a wire rack to cool completely.

For the Cream Cheese Filling:

Beat Cream Cheese and Butter:
- In a large bowl, beat together the softened cream cheese and butter until smooth and creamy.

Add Confectioners' Sugar and Vanilla:
- Add the confectioners' sugar and vanilla extract. Beat until well combined and smooth.

Assemble Whoopie Pies:
- Once the cookies are completely cooled, spread a generous amount of cream cheese filling on the flat side of one cookie. Top it with another cookie to create a sandwich.

Enjoy:
- Repeat with the remaining cookies and filling. Enjoy your Pumpkin Whoopie Pies!

Optional Tips:

- You can add a pinch of ground cloves or allspice to the cookie batter for extra warmth and flavor.
- If you like, roll the assembled whoopie pies in chopped nuts, shredded coconut, or decorative sprinkles for added texture and appearance.
- Store the whoopie pies in the refrigerator if you prefer a firmer filling, especially if the ambient temperature is warm.

These Pumpkin Whoopie Pies are perfect for fall or any time you're craving the delicious combination of pumpkin and cream cheese. They make a festive and tasty addition to holiday gatherings or as a sweet treat for family and friends.

New England Apple Cider Donut Holes

Ingredients:

For the Donut Holes:

- 2 cups apple cider
- 2 cups all-purpose flour
- 1 1/2 teaspoons baking powder
- 1/2 teaspoon baking soda
- 1/2 teaspoon salt
- 1 teaspoon ground cinnamon
- 1/4 teaspoon ground nutmeg
- 1/4 cup unsalted butter, softened
- 1/2 cup granulated sugar
- 1/4 cup brown sugar, packed
- 2 large eggs
- 1 teaspoon vanilla extract
- Vegetable oil for frying

For the Cinnamon Sugar Coating:

- 1 cup granulated sugar
- 1 tablespoon ground cinnamon

Instructions:

For the Donut Holes:

Reduce Apple Cider:
- In a saucepan over medium heat, bring the apple cider to a simmer. Reduce it to 1/2 cup by simmering for about 15-20 minutes. Allow it to cool.

Whisk Dry Ingredients:
- In a bowl, whisk together the flour, baking powder, baking soda, salt, cinnamon, and nutmeg. Set aside.

Cream Butter and Sugars:
- In a large bowl, cream together the softened butter, granulated sugar, and brown sugar until light and fluffy.

Add Eggs and Vanilla:

- Add the eggs one at a time, beating well after each addition. Stir in the vanilla extract.

Combine Dry and Wet Ingredients:
- Gradually add the dry ingredients to the wet ingredients, alternating with the reduced apple cider. Begin and end with the dry ingredients. Mix until just combined. Do not overmix.

Chill Dough:
- Cover the dough and chill it in the refrigerator for at least 1 hour.

Heat Oil:
- Heat vegetable oil in a deep fryer or heavy-bottomed pot to 350°F (175°C).

Form Donut Holes:
- Scoop small portions of chilled dough and roll them into balls to form the donut holes.

Fry:
- Carefully drop the donut holes into the hot oil and fry until golden brown, turning them occasionally for even cooking. This should take about 2-3 minutes.

Drain and Cool:
- Use a slotted spoon to transfer the fried donut holes to a paper towel-lined plate to drain excess oil. Allow them to cool slightly.

For the Cinnamon Sugar Coating:

Combine Sugar and Cinnamon:
- In a bowl, combine granulated sugar and ground cinnamon for the coating.

Coat Donut Holes:
- While the donut holes are still warm, roll them in the cinnamon sugar mixture until evenly coated.

Serve and Enjoy:
- Serve the Apple Cider Donut Holes warm and enjoy the delicious, spiced flavor.

Optional Tips:

- Feel free to add a touch of ground cloves or allspice to the cinnamon sugar coating for additional warmth.
- These donut holes are best enjoyed on the day they are made for optimal freshness.

- For a fun twist, you can also glaze the donut holes with a simple apple cider glaze made with powdered sugar and reduced apple cider.

These New England Apple Cider Donut Holes capture the essence of fall with their warm, spiced flavors. They make for a delightful treat for autumn gatherings, cozy weekends, or any time you want to savor the taste of apple cider and cinnamon.

Baked Beans with Maple Syrup

Ingredients:

- 1 pound dried navy beans or white beans
- Water for soaking and cooking
- 1 large onion, finely chopped
- 1/2 cup molasses
- 1/4 cup pure maple syrup
- 1/4 cup brown sugar, packed
- 1/4 cup ketchup
- 1 tablespoon Dijon mustard
- 1 teaspoon salt
- 1/4 teaspoon black pepper
- 4 cups water (for cooking beans)
- 4 cups chicken or vegetable broth (or additional water)
- 1/4 pound salt pork or bacon, cut into small pieces (optional)

Instructions:

Soak Beans:
- Rinse the dried beans thoroughly and place them in a large bowl. Cover the beans with water and let them soak overnight. Alternatively, you can use the quick soak method by boiling the beans for 2 minutes, then letting them soak for 1 hour.

Preheat Oven:
- Preheat your oven to 325°F (163°C).

Cook Beans:
- Drain the soaked beans and place them in a large pot. Add 4 cups of water and bring to a boil. Reduce the heat to a simmer and cook the beans for about 30 minutes or until they are partially cooked. Drain the beans.

Prepare Maple Syrup Mixture:
- In a bowl, mix together the chopped onion, molasses, maple syrup, brown sugar, ketchup, Dijon mustard, salt, and black pepper.

Combine Beans and Mixture:
- In a baking dish or Dutch oven, combine the partially cooked beans and the maple syrup mixture. If you're using salt pork or bacon, distribute the pieces throughout the beans.

Add Broth:

- Pour in the chicken or vegetable broth (or additional water) until the beans are just covered.

Bake:
- Cover the baking dish or Dutch oven with a lid or aluminum foil. Bake in the preheated oven for 4-6 hours or until the beans are tender, stirring occasionally. Add more liquid if needed during the baking process.

Finish Cooking:
- If you prefer a thicker consistency, uncover the beans during the last hour of cooking to allow the liquid to reduce.

Serve:
- Once the beans are tender and the sauce has thickened to your liking, remove them from the oven. Let them cool slightly before serving.

Enjoy:
- Serve the Baked Beans with Maple Syrup as a side dish to your favorite meals.

Optional Tips:

- You can add a smoky flavor by including a small amount of smoked ham or using smoked bacon.
- For extra richness, you can stir in a couple of tablespoons of unsalted butter before serving.
- Adjust the sweetness and tanginess to your liking by tweaking the amounts of maple syrup, molasses, and brown sugar.

Baked Beans with Maple Syrup is a comforting and flavorful dish that's perfect for gatherings, barbecues, or a cozy night at home. The combination of maple syrup and molasses gives the beans a deliciously sweet and robust flavor.

Cape Codder Cocktail

Ingredients:

- 1 1/2 ounces vodka
- 4 ounces cranberry juice
- Ice cubes
- Fresh lime wedge or twist, for garnish (optional)

Instructions:

Fill Glass with Ice:
- Fill a highball glass with ice cubes.

Add Vodka:
- Pour the vodka over the ice in the glass.

Pour Cranberry Juice:
- Pour the cranberry juice over the vodka and ice.

Stir:
- Gently stir the ingredients in the glass to mix the vodka and cranberry juice.

Garnish (Optional):
- Garnish the cocktail with a fresh lime wedge or twist if desired.

Serve and Enjoy:
- Serve the Cape Codder Cocktail immediately and enjoy the refreshing combination of cranberry and vodka.

Optional Tips:

- If you prefer a sweeter version, you can use cranberry juice cocktail instead of pure cranberry juice. Adjust the amount of cranberry juice to your taste.
- Consider using flavored vodka, such as citrus or raspberry, for an extra layer of flavor.
- To make a larger batch for a gathering, you can mix vodka and cranberry juice in a pitcher, and guests can serve themselves over ice.

The Cape Codder Cocktail is a simple yet classic drink that's perfect for summer, brunch, or any occasion where you crave a vibrant and fruity beverage. The combination of cranberry juice and vodka makes for a visually appealing and deliciously tart cocktail.

Grilled Swordfish Steaks

Ingredients:

- 4 swordfish steaks, about 1 inch thick
- 3 tablespoons olive oil
- 2 tablespoons lemon juice
- 2 cloves garlic, minced
- 1 teaspoon dried oregano
- Salt and black pepper, to taste
- Lemon wedges and fresh herbs for garnish (optional)

Instructions:

Prepare the Swordfish:
- Pat the swordfish steaks dry with paper towels. This helps ensure a better sear on the grill.

Marinate the Swordfish:
- In a bowl, whisk together the olive oil, lemon juice, minced garlic, dried oregano, salt, and black pepper to create a marinade. Place the swordfish steaks in a shallow dish and pour the marinade over them. Let them marinate for at least 15-30 minutes, allowing the flavors to infuse.

Preheat the Grill:
- Preheat your grill to medium-high heat. Make sure the grates are clean and well-oiled to prevent sticking.

Grill the Swordfish:
- Remove the swordfish steaks from the marinade and let any excess marinade drip off. Place the steaks on the preheated grill.

Grill Time:
- Grill the swordfish for about 4-5 minutes per side, or until the fish is opaque and easily flakes with a fork. The total grilling time will depend on the thickness of the steaks.

Baste (Optional):
- If you want to add extra flavor, you can baste the swordfish with any remaining marinade during the grilling process.

Check for Doneness:
- Use a fork to check the doneness of the swordfish. The flesh should be opaque and easily separate into flakes.

Serve:

- Transfer the grilled swordfish steaks to a serving platter. Garnish with lemon wedges and fresh herbs if desired.

Enjoy:
- Serve the grilled swordfish steaks immediately and enjoy the delicious, smoky flavors.

Optional Tips:

- If using wooden skewers, soak them in water for 30 minutes before grilling to prevent burning.
- Swordfish pairs well with various side dishes such as grilled vegetables, rice, or a fresh salad.
- Experiment with different marinade variations by adding herbs like thyme or rosemary, or a splash of your favorite citrus juice.

Grilled swordfish is a versatile dish that can be served as a main course for a weeknight dinner or as a centerpiece for a special occasion. The simple marinade enhances the natural flavors of the fish while giving it a delicious Mediterranean-inspired twist.

Bluefish Pate

Ingredients:

- 1 cup cooked bluefish, flaked and deboned
- 4 ounces cream cheese, softened
- 2 tablespoons mayonnaise
- 1 tablespoon Dijon mustard
- 1 tablespoon lemon juice
- 1 tablespoon fresh parsley, chopped
- 1 green onion, finely chopped
- Salt and black pepper, to taste
- Crackers or sliced baguette, for serving

Instructions:

Prepare Bluefish:
- Cook the bluefish by grilling, baking, or poaching it until fully cooked. Allow it to cool, then flake the fish and remove any bones.

Combine Ingredients:
- In a bowl, combine the flaked bluefish, softened cream cheese, mayonnaise, Dijon mustard, lemon juice, chopped parsley, and chopped green onion.

Season:
- Season the mixture with salt and black pepper to taste. Remember that the fish may already have some saltiness, so adjust accordingly.

Blend:
- Use a hand mixer or food processor to blend the ingredients until smooth and well combined. Taste and adjust the seasoning if needed.

Chill:
- Transfer the bluefish pate to a serving dish or individual ramekins. Cover and refrigerate for at least 1-2 hours to allow the flavors to meld.

Serve:
- Serve the chilled bluefish pate with crackers or sliced baguette.

Optional Tips:

- Add a touch of hot sauce or cayenne pepper for a bit of heat.

- Garnish the top of the pate with additional chopped parsley, chives, or a sprinkle of paprika for a decorative touch.
- If you have smoked bluefish, it can add an extra layer of flavor to the pate.

This Bluefish Pate is a flavorful and unique way to enjoy this rich and oily fish. It's perfect for gatherings, picnics, or as an appetizer for seafood lovers. Adjust the ingredients to your taste preferences and enjoy the delicious spread on your favorite crackers or bread.

New England Harvest Salad

Ingredients:

For the Salad:

- 6 cups mixed salad greens (e.g., spinach, arugula, and/or mixed baby lettuces)
- 1 cup sliced apples (such as Honeycrisp or Gala)
- 1 cup sliced pears (such as Bosc or Anjou)
- 1/2 cup dried cranberries
- 1/2 cup chopped pecans or walnuts, toasted
- 1/2 cup crumbled goat cheese or feta
- 1/4 cup thinly sliced red onion
- 1/4 cup pomegranate seeds (optional)

For the Maple Dijon Vinaigrette:

- 1/4 cup olive oil
- 2 tablespoons apple cider vinegar
- 1 tablespoon maple syrup
- 1 teaspoon Dijon mustard
- Salt and black pepper, to taste

Instructions:

Prepare the Salad Greens:
- In a large salad bowl, combine the mixed salad greens.

Add Fruits and Nuts:
- Add the sliced apples, sliced pears, dried cranberries, toasted pecans or walnuts, and thinly sliced red onion to the salad greens.

Sprinkle Cheese and Pomegranate Seeds:
- Sprinkle crumbled goat cheese or feta over the salad. If using, add pomegranate seeds for an extra burst of flavor.

Prepare the Maple Dijon Vinaigrette:
- In a small bowl or jar, whisk together olive oil, apple cider vinegar, maple syrup, Dijon mustard, salt, and black pepper. Adjust the seasoning to taste.

Dress the Salad:

- Drizzle the Maple Dijon Vinaigrette over the salad. Toss gently to coat the ingredients evenly.

Serve:
- Transfer the salad to individual plates or a serving platter. Optionally, garnish with additional nuts or cheese.

Enjoy:
- Serve the New England Harvest Salad immediately and enjoy the vibrant flavors of fall.

Optional Tips:

- Customize the salad by adding roasted butternut squash or sweet potatoes for additional autumn flavors.
- Experiment with different varieties of apples and pears to explore diverse tastes and textures.
- For extra protein, you can add grilled chicken or roasted turkey slices.

This New England Harvest Salad is not only visually appealing with its autumn colors but also a delicious and nutritious way to celebrate the flavors of the season. The combination of crisp apples, juicy pears, and sweet cranberries creates a refreshing and satisfying salad perfect for any fall occasion.

Apple Cider Chicken

Ingredients:

- 4 boneless, skinless chicken breasts
- Salt and black pepper, to taste
- 2 tablespoons olive oil
- 1 onion, thinly sliced
- 2 cloves garlic, minced
- 1 teaspoon dried thyme
- 1 teaspoon dried rosemary
- 1/2 teaspoon ground cinnamon
- 1/2 teaspoon ground nutmeg
- 1 cup apple cider
- 1/2 cup chicken broth
- 2 tablespoons Dijon mustard
- 2 tablespoons maple syrup
- Fresh parsley, chopped, for garnish (optional)

Instructions:

Season Chicken:
- Season the chicken breasts with salt and black pepper on both sides.

Sear Chicken:
- In a large skillet, heat olive oil over medium-high heat. Add the chicken breasts and sear until golden brown on both sides. Remove the chicken from the skillet and set aside.

Sauté Onion and Garlic:
- In the same skillet, add sliced onion and sauté until softened. Add minced garlic and cook for an additional 1-2 minutes until fragrant.

Add Herbs and Spices:
- Stir in dried thyme, dried rosemary, ground cinnamon, and ground nutmeg. Cook for another 1-2 minutes to toast the spices.

Deglaze with Apple Cider:
- Pour in the apple cider and chicken broth, using a spatula to scrape up any browned bits from the bottom of the skillet.

Combine Mustard and Maple Syrup:

- In a small bowl, whisk together Dijon mustard and maple syrup. Add the mixture to the skillet and stir well.

Return Chicken to Skillet:
- Return the seared chicken breasts to the skillet, nestling them into the sauce.

Simmer:
- Reduce the heat to medium-low and let the chicken simmer in the sauce for about 15-20 minutes or until the chicken is cooked through and the sauce has thickened.

Garnish (Optional):
- Garnish with chopped fresh parsley if desired.

Serve:
- Serve the Apple Cider Chicken over rice, mashed potatoes, or with your favorite side dishes.

Optional Tips:

- For an extra layer of flavor, you can add sliced apples to the skillet along with the onions.
- If you prefer bone-in chicken, you can use chicken thighs or drumsticks for this recipe.
- Adjust the sweetness and tanginess by modifying the amount of maple syrup and Dijon mustard to suit your taste.

This Apple Cider Chicken recipe offers a delightful combination of savory and sweet flavors, making it a perfect dish for autumn or any time you want a comforting and delicious meal.

Cranberry Chutney

Ingredients:

- 1 bag (12 ounces) fresh or frozen cranberries
- 1 cup granulated sugar
- 1/2 cup brown sugar, packed
- 1/2 cup water
- 1 medium apple, peeled, cored, and diced
- 1 medium orange, zest and juice
- 1/2 cup raisins or currants
- 1/2 cup chopped pecans or walnuts (optional)
- 1 teaspoon ground cinnamon
- 1/2 teaspoon ground ginger
- 1/4 teaspoon ground cloves
- Pinch of salt

Instructions:

Combine Ingredients:
- In a medium-sized saucepan, combine the fresh or frozen cranberries, granulated sugar, brown sugar, water, diced apple, orange zest, and orange juice.

Cook Over Medium Heat:
- Bring the mixture to a simmer over medium heat, stirring occasionally.

Add Remaining Ingredients:
- Once the cranberries begin to burst and the mixture thickens slightly, add raisins or currants, chopped nuts (if using), ground cinnamon, ground ginger, ground cloves, and a pinch of salt.

Simmer:
- Continue to simmer the chutney over medium-low heat, stirring occasionally, until it reaches your desired consistency. This usually takes about 15-20 minutes.

Adjust Sweetness:
- Taste the chutney and adjust the sweetness by adding more sugar if needed.

Cool:
- Remove the saucepan from heat and allow the cranberry chutney to cool.

Store:

- Transfer the cooled cranberry chutney to a jar or airtight container and refrigerate until ready to use. It will continue to thicken as it cools.

Serve:
- Serve the cranberry chutney as a side dish with roasted turkey or chicken, spread it on sandwiches, or use it as a condiment for cheese platters.

Optional Tips:

- Add a splash of orange liqueur or brandy for an extra layer of flavor.
- Customize the chutney by incorporating diced pears, grated ginger, or a pinch of cayenne pepper for a hint of heat.
- Adjust the texture by cooking the chutney for a shorter time for a chunkier consistency or longer for a smoother, jam-like texture.

This Cranberry Chutney is a versatile and vibrant addition to your holiday table, bringing a balance of sweet, tart, and spicy flavors. It's a delightful accompaniment to a variety of dishes and adds a festive touch to your meals.

Boston Cream Pie Trifle

Ingredients:

For the Vanilla Custard:

- 2 cups whole milk
- 1/2 cup granulated sugar
- 1/4 cup cornstarch
- Pinch of salt
- 4 large egg yolks
- 2 teaspoons vanilla extract

For the Trifle:

- 1 store-bought or homemade pound cake, cut into cubes
- 1 cup chocolate ganache (made with equal parts chocolate and heavy cream)
- 1 cup whipped cream or whipped topping

Instructions:

For the Vanilla Custard:

Prepare Ingredients:
- In a bowl, whisk together the sugar, cornstarch, and salt. Set aside.

Heat Milk:
- In a saucepan, heat the milk over medium heat until it just starts to simmer. Do not let it boil.

Temper Egg Yolks:
- In a separate bowl, whisk the egg yolks. Slowly whisk in the sugar-cornstarch mixture. Gradually pour in a small amount of the hot milk into the egg mixture while whisking constantly (tempering the eggs).

Cook Custard:
- Pour the tempered egg mixture back into the saucepan with the remaining hot milk. Cook over medium heat, whisking constantly, until the mixture thickens and comes to a boil.

Add Vanilla:
- Remove from heat and stir in the vanilla extract. Let the custard cool to room temperature or refrigerate until ready to use.

Assembling the Trifle:

- Layer Pound Cake:
  - In a trifle dish or individual serving glasses, start with a layer of pound cake cubes.
- Add Custard:
  - Spoon a layer of vanilla custard over the pound cake.
- Drizzle Ganache:
  - Drizzle a layer of chocolate ganache over the custard.
- Repeat Layers:
  - Repeat the layers until you reach the top of the trifle dish or glasses, finishing with a layer of whipped cream.
- Chill:
  - Refrigerate the Boston Cream Pie Trifle for at least 2 hours to allow the flavors to meld and the dessert to set.
- Serve:
  - Before serving, you can garnish the top with additional chocolate ganache, whipped cream, or chocolate shavings if desired.

Optional Tips:

- For a homemade pound cake, you can use a classic vanilla pound cake or experiment with other flavors like lemon or almond.
- Adjust the sweetness by adding more or less sugar to the vanilla custard, depending on your preference.
- Feel free to customize the trifle by adding sliced strawberries, bananas, or a layer of pastry cream.

This Boston Cream Pie Trifle is a luscious and visually stunning dessert that brings together the beloved flavors of Boston Cream Pie in a delightful layered form. It's perfect for special occasions or any time you want to impress with a delicious and elegant treat.

Lobster Bisque

Ingredients:

- 2 lobsters (about 1.5 to 2 pounds each)
- 4 tablespoons unsalted butter
- 1 onion, chopped
- 1 carrot, chopped
- 2 celery stalks, chopped
- 2 cloves garlic, minced
- 1/4 cup all-purpose flour
- 1/4 cup tomato paste
- 1 cup dry white wine
- 4 cups fish or seafood stock
- 2 cups chicken broth
- 1 bay leaf
- 1 teaspoon paprika
- 1/2 teaspoon cayenne pepper (adjust to taste)
- Salt and black pepper, to taste
- 2 cups heavy cream
- Chopped fresh parsley, for garnish
- Lobster meat for garnish (optional)

Instructions:

Prepare Lobsters:
- Bring a large pot of salted water to a boil. Cook the lobsters for about 8-10 minutes or until they turn bright red. Remove the lobsters and let them cool. Once cool, remove the meat from the shells, reserving some for garnish if desired. Chop the lobster meat into bite-sized pieces.

Make Lobster Stock:
- Break the lobster shells into smaller pieces. In a large pot, melt 2 tablespoons of butter over medium heat. Add the lobster shells and cook for about 5-7 minutes until they release their flavors. Add the chopped onion, carrot, celery, and garlic. Cook for an additional 5-7 minutes until the vegetables soften.

Add Tomato Paste:
- Stir in the tomato paste and cook for 2-3 minutes to caramelize it slightly.

Deglaze with Wine:

- Pour in the white wine, scraping the bottom of the pot to release any flavorful bits. Simmer for a few minutes to reduce the wine.

Add Broths and Seasonings:
- Add the fish or seafood stock, chicken broth, bay leaf, paprika, cayenne pepper, salt, and black pepper. Bring the mixture to a simmer and let it cook for about 20-30 minutes to develop flavors.

Strain the Stock:
- Strain the stock through a fine-mesh strainer or cheesecloth into a clean bowl, discarding the solids. You should have a rich lobster broth.

Make the Bisque:
- In the same pot, melt the remaining 2 tablespoons of butter over medium heat. Stir in the flour to create a roux. Cook for 2-3 minutes, stirring constantly.

Add Lobster Broth:
- Gradually whisk in the lobster broth to the roux, ensuring there are no lumps. Continue whisking until the mixture thickens.

Blend and Simmer:
- Use an immersion blender to blend the soup until smooth. Alternatively, transfer the mixture to a blender and blend in batches. Return the soup to the pot and simmer for an additional 10 minutes.

Add Cream and Lobster Meat:
- Stir in the heavy cream and add the chopped lobster meat. Simmer for another 5-7 minutes until the lobster is heated through and the bisque is rich and creamy.

Adjust Seasoning:
- Taste and adjust the seasoning, adding more salt, pepper, or cayenne if needed.

Serve:
- Ladle the lobster bisque into bowls. Garnish with chopped fresh parsley and additional lobster meat if desired.

Enjoy this luxurious and flavorful Lobster Bisque as a starter for a special dinner or as a comforting treat on a chilly evening.

Maple Glazed Sweet Potatoes

Ingredients:

- 4 medium-sized sweet potatoes, peeled and cut into cubes
- 3 tablespoons unsalted butter, melted
- 1/4 cup pure maple syrup
- 1 teaspoon ground cinnamon
- 1/2 teaspoon ground nutmeg
- 1/2 teaspoon salt
- 1/4 teaspoon black pepper
- Chopped fresh parsley or pecans for garnish (optional)

Instructions:

Preheat Oven:
- Preheat your oven to 375°F (190°C).

Prepare Sweet Potatoes:
- Peel the sweet potatoes and cut them into evenly sized cubes.

Mix Glaze:
- In a bowl, mix together melted butter, maple syrup, ground cinnamon, ground nutmeg, salt, and black pepper.

Coat Sweet Potatoes:
- Place the sweet potato cubes in a large bowl and pour the maple glaze over them. Toss the sweet potatoes until they are evenly coated with the glaze.

Bake:
- Transfer the coated sweet potatoes to a baking dish or a parchment-lined baking sheet, spreading them out in a single layer.

Roast:
- Roast in the preheated oven for about 30-40 minutes or until the sweet potatoes are tender, stirring occasionally to ensure even coating.

Garnish (Optional):
- If desired, garnish the Maple Glazed Sweet Potatoes with chopped fresh parsley or pecans for an extra touch.

Serve:
- Transfer the sweet potatoes to a serving dish and serve warm.

Optional Tips:

- Add a pinch of cayenne pepper for a subtle kick or a sprinkle of orange zest for a citrusy twist.
- If you prefer a sweeter glaze, you can increase the amount of maple syrup or add a bit of brown sugar.
- Experiment with different herbs and spices, such as thyme or smoked paprika, to add depth of flavor.

These Maple Glazed Sweet Potatoes make for a delightful and comforting side dish. The natural sweetness of the sweet potatoes combined with the richness of maple syrup creates a dish that's sure to be a hit at your table. Enjoy them alongside your favorite main courses.

Blueberry Lemon Scones

Ingredients:

- 2 cups all-purpose flour
- 1/4 cup granulated sugar
- 1 tablespoon baking powder
- 1/2 teaspoon salt
- Zest of 1 lemon
- 1/2 cup unsalted butter, cold and cut into small pieces
- 1 cup fresh or frozen blueberries
- 1/2 cup milk (plus extra for brushing)
- 1 large egg
- 1 teaspoon vanilla extract
- Optional: Turbinado sugar for sprinkling on top

Instructions:

Preheat Oven:
- Preheat your oven to 400°F (200°C). Line a baking sheet with parchment paper.

Combine Dry Ingredients:
- In a large bowl, whisk together the flour, sugar, baking powder, salt, and lemon zest.

Add Cold Butter:
- Add the cold, diced butter to the dry ingredients. Use a pastry cutter or your fingers to cut the butter into the flour mixture until it resembles coarse crumbs.

Incorporate Blueberries:
- Gently fold in the blueberries, trying not to crush them.

Whisk Wet Ingredients:
- In a separate bowl, whisk together the milk, egg, and vanilla extract.

Combine Wet and Dry Mixtures:
- Pour the wet ingredients into the dry ingredients and stir until just combined. Be careful not to overmix.

Shape the Dough:
- Turn the dough out onto a lightly floured surface and gently knead it a few times to bring it together. Pat the dough into a circle about 1 inch (2.5 cm) thick.

Cut into Wedges:
- Using a sharp knife, cut the dough into 8 wedges.

Arrange on Baking Sheet:
- Place the scones on the prepared baking sheet, leaving some space between each wedge.

Brush with Milk and Sugar (Optional):
- Brush the tops of the scones with a little milk and, if desired, sprinkle with turbinado sugar for a nice, sweet crunch.

Bake:
- Bake in the preheated oven for 15-18 minutes or until the tops are golden brown.

Cool:
- Allow the scones to cool on the baking sheet for a few minutes before transferring them to a wire rack to cool completely.

Serve:
- Once cooled, serve the Blueberry Lemon Scones and enjoy!

Optional Tips:

- If using frozen blueberries, toss them in a little flour before adding them to the batter to prevent them from sinking to the bottom.
- For an extra lemony kick, you can add a simple lemon glaze made with powdered sugar and lemon juice once the scones have cooled.

These Blueberry Lemon Scones are tender, flaky, and bursting with flavor. They are a delightful addition to your morning routine or afternoon tea.

Boston Brown Bread Ice Cream Sandwiches

Ingredients:

For the Boston Brown Bread Cookies:

- 1 cup cornmeal
- 1 cup whole wheat flour
- 1 cup all-purpose flour
- 1 teaspoon baking soda
- 1/2 teaspoon salt
- 1 cup buttermilk
- 1/2 cup molasses
- 1/4 cup brown sugar
- 1/4 cup unsalted butter, melted
- 1/2 cup raisins (optional)

For Assembling the Ice Cream Sandwiches:

- Your favorite vanilla ice cream

Instructions:

For the Boston Brown Bread Cookies:

Preheat Oven:
- Preheat your oven to 350°F (175°C). Line a baking sheet with parchment paper.

Mix Dry Ingredients:
- In a large bowl, whisk together the cornmeal, whole wheat flour, all-purpose flour, baking soda, and salt.

Combine Wet Ingredients:
- In another bowl, mix together the buttermilk, molasses, brown sugar, and melted butter until well combined.

Combine Wet and Dry Mixtures:
- Pour the wet ingredients into the dry ingredients and stir until just combined. If using, fold in the raisins.

Shape Cookies:
- Drop spoonfuls of dough onto the prepared baking sheet, forming round cookie shapes.

Bake:
- Bake in the preheated oven for about 10-12 minutes or until the edges are set. The cookies will be soft but will firm up as they cool.

Cool:
- Allow the cookies to cool on the baking sheet for a few minutes before transferring them to a wire rack to cool completely.

For Assembling the Ice Cream Sandwiches:

Prepare Cookies:
- Once the cookies have cooled completely, pair them up to create sandwich pairs.

Add Ice Cream:
- Take a scoop of your favorite vanilla ice cream and place it on the bottom side of one cookie. Top with the matching cookie, pressing down gently to create a sandwich.

Freeze:
- Place the ice cream sandwiches in the freezer for at least 1-2 hours or until the ice cream is firm.

Serve:
- Once frozen, serve the Boston Brown Bread Ice Cream Sandwiches and enjoy!

Optional Tips:

- Experiment with different ice cream flavors to create unique combinations.
- Roll the edges of the ice cream sandwiches in chopped nuts, chocolate chips, or sprinkles for added texture.
- Store the assembled sandwiches in an airtight container in the freezer for longer storage.

These Boston Brown Bread Ice Cream Sandwiches are a fun and tasty way to enjoy the flavors of brown bread in a frozen treat. Perfect for a summer day or any time you crave a delightful ice cream sandwich with a unique twist.

Clam and Corn Fritters

Ingredients:

- 1 cup fresh or canned clams, drained and chopped
- 1 cup fresh or frozen corn kernels
- 1 cup all-purpose flour
- 1 teaspoon baking powder
- 1/2 teaspoon Old Bay seasoning (optional)
- 1/2 teaspoon salt
- 1/4 teaspoon black pepper
- 2 large eggs
- 1/2 cup milk
- 2 green onions, finely chopped
- 2 tablespoons fresh parsley, chopped
- Vegetable oil for frying
- Lemon wedges for serving

Instructions:

Prepare Clams and Corn:
- If using fresh clams, ensure they are shucked, cleaned, and chopped. If using canned clams, drain them well. Thaw frozen corn if using.

Mix Dry Ingredients:
- In a large bowl, whisk together the flour, baking powder, Old Bay seasoning (if using), salt, and black pepper.

Combine Wet Ingredients:
- In another bowl, beat the eggs and stir in the milk.

Combine Mixtures:
- Pour the wet ingredients into the dry ingredients and mix until just combined.

Add Clams, Corn, and Herbs:
- Fold in the chopped clams, corn kernels, green onions, and fresh parsley. The batter should be thick and chunky.

Heat Oil:
- In a large skillet, heat vegetable oil over medium-high heat until it reaches 350°F (180°C).

Fry Fritters:

- Drop spoonfuls of the batter into the hot oil, flattening them slightly with the back of the spoon. Fry until the fritters are golden brown on both sides, about 2-3 minutes per side.

Drain Excess Oil:
- Remove the fritters with a slotted spoon and place them on a paper towel-lined plate to drain any excess oil.

Serve:
- Serve the Clam and Corn Fritters warm with lemon wedges on the side.

Optional Tips:

- For added heat, you can add a pinch of cayenne pepper or a dash of hot sauce to the batter.
- Experiment with different herbs and spices based on your preferences.
- Serve the fritters with a dipping sauce, such as tartar sauce or aioli, for extra flavor.

These Clam and Corn Fritters make for a delicious appetizer or snack, showcasing the flavors of the sea and the sweetness of corn in every crispy bite. Enjoy them on their own or with your favorite dipping sauce.

Boston Cream Pie Pancakes

Ingredients:

For the Pancakes:

- 1 cup all-purpose flour
- 2 tablespoons granulated sugar
- 1 teaspoon baking powder
- 1/2 teaspoon baking soda
- 1/4 teaspoon salt
- 3/4 cup buttermilk
- 1/4 cup milk
- 1 large egg
- 2 tablespoons unsalted butter, melted
- 1 teaspoon vanilla extract

For the Filling:

- 1 cup vanilla pudding or pastry cream (homemade or store-bought)

For the Chocolate Ganache:

- 1/2 cup semi-sweet chocolate chips
- 1/4 cup heavy cream
- 1 tablespoon unsalted butter

Instructions:

For the Pancakes:

Preheat Griddle or Pan:
- Preheat a griddle or non-stick pan over medium heat.

Mix Dry Ingredients:
- In a large bowl, whisk together the flour, sugar, baking powder, baking soda, and salt.

Combine Wet Ingredients:
- In another bowl, whisk together the buttermilk, milk, egg, melted butter, and vanilla extract.

Combine Mixtures:

- Pour the wet ingredients into the dry ingredients and stir until just combined. Be careful not to overmix; it's okay if there are a few lumps.

Cook Pancakes:
- Spoon the batter onto the preheated griddle to form pancakes. Cook until bubbles form on the surface, then flip and cook until the other side is golden brown.

Keep Warm:
- Keep the cooked pancakes warm while you prepare the filling and ganache.

For the Filling:

Prepare Vanilla Pudding or Pastry Cream:
- Prepare the vanilla pudding or pastry cream according to the recipe instructions or use store-bought.

For the Chocolate Ganache:

Make Chocolate Ganache:
- In a small saucepan, heat the heavy cream until it just starts to simmer. Remove from heat and add the chocolate chips and butter. Let it sit for a minute, then stir until smooth and glossy.

Assemble Pancakes:
- To assemble, spread a layer of vanilla pudding or pastry cream on one pancake and top with another pancake to create a sandwich.

Drizzle with Ganache:
- Drizzle the chocolate ganache over the top of the pancake sandwiches.

Serve:
- Serve the Boston Cream Pie Pancakes warm and enjoy!

Optional Tips:

- You can add a touch of sweetness to the pancake batter by incorporating a tablespoon of sugar or using sweetened buttermilk.
- Customize the filling by using chocolate or vanilla-flavored whipped cream instead of vanilla pudding.
- Garnish the pancakes with sliced strawberries, bananas, or a dusting of powdered sugar for extra flavor and presentation.

These Boston Cream Pie Pancakes bring the delightful combination of creamy filling and chocolate ganache to your breakfast table. They're a delicious treat for special occasions or when you want to indulge in a sweet and satisfying morning meal.

Cranberry Walnut Chicken Salad

Ingredients:

- 2 cups cooked and shredded chicken (rotisserie chicken works well)
- 1/2 cup mayonnaise
- 1/4 cup Greek yogurt or sour cream
- 1 tablespoon Dijon mustard
- 1 tablespoon honey
- 1/2 cup dried cranberries
- 1/2 cup chopped walnuts, toasted
- 2 celery stalks, finely chopped
- 2 green onions, thinly sliced
- Salt and black pepper, to taste
- Fresh parsley for garnish (optional)

Instructions:

Prepare Chicken:
- Cook and shred the chicken. You can use leftover roasted or grilled chicken, or a rotisserie chicken for convenience.

Toast Walnuts:
- In a dry skillet over medium heat, toast the chopped walnuts for a few minutes until they become fragrant. Stir frequently to avoid burning. Remove from heat and let them cool.

Make Dressing:
- In a large bowl, whisk together mayonnaise, Greek yogurt or sour cream, Dijon mustard, and honey until well combined.

Combine Ingredients:
- Add the shredded chicken, dried cranberries, toasted walnuts, chopped celery, and sliced green onions to the bowl.

Mix and Season:
- Gently toss all the ingredients until evenly coated with the dressing. Season with salt and black pepper to taste.

Chill:
- Cover the bowl and refrigerate the Cranberry Walnut Chicken Salad for at least 30 minutes to allow the flavors to meld.

Serve:

- Before serving, give the salad a final toss. Garnish with fresh parsley if desired.

Enjoy:
- Serve the Cranberry Walnut Chicken Salad on a bed of lettuce, in a sandwich, or with crackers. Enjoy!

Optional Tips:

- For added freshness, you can incorporate diced apples or grapes into the salad.
- Adjust the sweetness by modifying the amount of honey to suit your taste.
- Include a dash of lemon juice or apple cider vinegar for a touch of acidity.

This Cranberry Walnut Chicken Salad is perfect for sandwiches, wraps, or as a light and satisfying salad. The combination of sweet and savory flavors, along with the crunch of walnuts, makes it a versatile and delicious dish for any occasion.

New England Pot Roast Sandwiches

Ingredients:

For the Pot Roast:

- 3-4 pounds beef chuck roast
- Salt and black pepper, to taste
- 2 tablespoons vegetable oil
- 1 large onion, sliced
- 3 cloves garlic, minced
- 1 cup beef broth
- 1 cup red wine (or additional beef broth)
- 2 tablespoons tomato paste
- 2 teaspoons Worcestershire sauce
- 1 teaspoon dried thyme
- 1 teaspoon dried rosemary
- 2 bay leaves
- Carrots and potatoes, peeled and cut into chunks (optional)

For the Sandwiches:

- Hoagie rolls or sandwich buns
- Sliced Swiss or provolone cheese (optional)
- Prepared horseradish sauce or Dijon mustard (optional)

Instructions:

For the Pot Roast:

Preheat Oven:
- Preheat your oven to 325°F (163°C).

Season and Brown the Roast:
- Season the chuck roast with salt and black pepper. In a large oven-safe pot or Dutch oven, heat the vegetable oil over medium-high heat. Brown the roast on all sides.

Saute Onions and Garlic:

- Add the sliced onions to the pot and sauté until they are softened. Add minced garlic and cook for an additional minute.

Combine Ingredients:
- In a bowl, mix together beef broth, red wine, tomato paste, Worcestershire sauce, dried thyme, dried rosemary, and bay leaves.

Add Liquid Mixture:
- Pour the liquid mixture over the roast and onions in the pot. If desired, add carrots and potatoes.

Braise in the Oven:
- Cover the pot and transfer it to the preheated oven. Braise for 3-4 hours or until the meat is tender and easily falls apart.

Shred Meat:
- Once cooked, shred the pot roast using two forks. Remove and discard the bay leaves.

For the Sandwiches:

Prepare Sandwich Rolls:
- Split the hoagie rolls or sandwich buns and toast them lightly.

Assemble Sandwiches:
- Pile the shredded pot roast onto the rolls. Optionally, add sliced Swiss or provolone cheese.

Optional Toppings:
- Spread prepared horseradish sauce or Dijon mustard on the rolls for an extra kick.

Serve:
- Serve the New England Pot Roast Sandwiches warm, with the au jus from the pot roast for dipping.

Optional Tips:

- For added flavor, sauté mushrooms and add them to the pot roast during the last hour of cooking.
- If you prefer a thicker sauce, you can mix 2 tablespoons of flour with water to create a slurry and stir it into the pot roast during the last 30 minutes of cooking.

These New England Pot Roast Sandwiches are a comforting and satisfying meal, perfect for a cozy dinner or lunch. The slow-cooked, tender pot roast combined with the savory au jus makes for a delicious and hearty sandwich experience.

Maple Glazed Brussels Sprouts

Ingredients:

- 1 pound Brussels sprouts, trimmed and halved
- 2 tablespoons olive oil
- Salt and black pepper, to taste
- 2 tablespoons pure maple syrup
- 1 tablespoon balsamic vinegar
- 1/4 cup chopped pecans or walnuts (optional)

Instructions:

Preheat Oven:
- Preheat your oven to 400°F (200°C).

Prepare Brussels Sprouts:
- Trim the ends of the Brussels sprouts and cut them in half.

Toss with Olive Oil:
- In a large bowl, toss the Brussels sprouts with olive oil until they are evenly coated. Season with salt and black pepper to taste.

Roast Brussels Sprouts:
- Spread the Brussels sprouts in a single layer on a baking sheet. Roast in the preheated oven for 20-25 minutes or until they are golden brown and crispy on the edges. Stir or shake the pan halfway through the cooking time for even roasting.

Prepare Glaze:
- In a small bowl, mix together maple syrup and balsamic vinegar.

Glaze Brussels Sprouts:
- Drizzle the maple-balsamic glaze over the roasted Brussels sprouts and toss to coat them evenly. If using nuts, add them at this stage.

Roast Again (Optional):
- Return the glazed Brussels sprouts to the oven for an additional 5-7 minutes or until the glaze has caramelized slightly.

Serve:
- Transfer the Maple Glazed Brussels Sprouts to a serving dish and serve immediately.

Optional Tips:

- Add a pinch of red pepper flakes for a touch of heat.
- Garnish with fresh chopped herbs, such as parsley or thyme, for extra flavor and freshness.
- If you prefer a stronger balsamic flavor, you can increase the amount of balsamic vinegar in the glaze.

These Maple Glazed Brussels Sprouts are a delicious side dish that pairs well with various main courses. The natural sweetness from the maple syrup and the tangy balsamic glaze elevate the Brussels sprouts to create a flavorful and irresistible dish.

Chow Mein Sandwich

Ingredients:

For the Chow Mein Filling:

- 1 tablespoon vegetable oil
- 1 onion, thinly sliced
- 2 cups shredded cabbage
- 1 cup julienned carrots
- 1 cup bean sprouts
- 1 cup sliced mushrooms
- 1 cup cooked and shredded chicken or beef (optional)
- 3 tablespoons soy sauce
- 2 tablespoons oyster sauce
- 1 tablespoon cornstarch mixed with 2 tablespoons water (optional, for thickening)

For the Sandwich:

- Sub rolls or sandwich buns

Instructions:

For the Chow Mein Filling:

    Stir-Fry Vegetables:
- Heat the vegetable oil in a large skillet or wok over medium-high heat. Add the sliced onion, shredded cabbage, julienned carrots, bean sprouts, and sliced mushrooms. Stir-fry for 5-7 minutes or until the vegetables are tender-crisp.

    Add Protein (Optional):
- If using chicken or beef, add the cooked and shredded meat to the vegetables. Stir to combine.

    Season with Sauces:
- Pour soy sauce and oyster sauce over the vegetable and meat mixture. Stir well to coat the ingredients evenly. If you prefer a thicker sauce, stir in the cornstarch-water mixture and cook until the sauce thickens.

    Cook:

- Continue cooking for an additional 2-3 minutes until the filling is heated through and well-coated with the sauce. Adjust the seasoning if needed.

For the Sandwich:

Prepare Buns:
- Slice the sub rolls or sandwich buns horizontally, leaving one side connected.

Fill Buns:
- Spoon the chow mein filling into the prepared buns, making sure to distribute the vegetables and protein evenly.

Serve:
- Serve the Chow Mein Sandwiches immediately, and enjoy this unique and flavorful creation!

Optional Tips:

- Customize the filling by adding your favorite vegetables or protein sources.
- For added heat, you can include a pinch of red pepper flakes or a dash of hot sauce.
- Top the Chow Mein Sandwich with sliced green onions or sesame seeds for extra flavor and garnish.

This Chow Mein Sandwich is a delicious and satisfying way to enjoy the flavors of chow mein in a handheld form. It's a creative fusion of Chinese and New England culinary influences that's sure to be a unique and tasty experience.

Boston Cream Pie Martini

Ingredients:

- 1 1/2 oz vanilla vodka
- 1 oz white chocolate liqueur
- 1 oz Godiva chocolate liqueur
- 1 oz half-and-half or heavy cream
- Chocolate syrup for garnish
- Cocoa powder for garnish

Instructions:

  Prepare Glass:
  - Drizzle chocolate syrup around the inside of a chilled martini glass. Swirl the glass to create a chocolate drizzle pattern.

  Chill Glass:
  - Place the prepared glass in the freezer while you make the cocktail to keep it cold.

  Shake Ingredients:
  - In a cocktail shaker filled with ice, combine the vanilla vodka, white chocolate liqueur, Godiva chocolate liqueur, and half-and-half or heavy cream.

  Shake Well:
  - Shake the ingredients well to chill the mixture and create a frothy texture.

  Strain into Glass:
  - Strain the cocktail into the chilled martini glass, being careful not to disturb the chocolate drizzle.

  Garnish:
  - Dust the top of the cocktail with a sprinkle of cocoa powder for an extra chocolate touch.

  Serve:
  - Serve the Boston Cream Pie Martini and enjoy this dessert-inspired cocktail!

Optional Tips:

- You can adjust the sweetness by adding more or less white chocolate liqueur or Godiva chocolate liqueur based on your preference.

- For an extra indulgent touch, rim the glass with crushed graham crackers or crushed chocolate cookies before drizzling with chocolate syrup.
- If you like your martinis extra cold, you can shake the cocktail for a longer time or add a few more ice cubes to the shaker.

This Boston Cream Pie Martini is a luscious and sweet cocktail that captures the essence of the classic dessert. It's perfect for a dessert-themed happy hour or as an indulgent treat for a special occasion. Enjoy responsibly!

Succotash

Ingredients:

- 2 cups fresh or frozen lima beans
- 2 cups fresh or frozen corn kernels
- 1 tablespoon butter
- 1 tablespoon olive oil
- 1 small onion, finely chopped
- 1 bell pepper (any color), diced
- 1-2 cloves garlic, minced
- Salt and black pepper, to taste
- 1 tablespoon fresh parsley, chopped (optional, for garnish)

Instructions:

Prepare Lima Beans and Corn:
- If using fresh lima beans, shell and prepare them. If using frozen, thaw according to package instructions. Likewise, if using fresh corn, remove the kernels from the cob. If using frozen, thaw.

Sauté Onion and Garlic:
- In a large skillet or pan, heat butter and olive oil over medium heat. Add finely chopped onion and sauté until translucent.

Add Bell Pepper:
- Add diced bell pepper to the skillet and cook until it starts to soften.

Combine Lima Beans and Corn:
- Stir in the lima beans and corn kernels, mixing them with the sautéed vegetables.

Season:
- Season the succotash with salt and black pepper to taste. You can also add other seasonings like paprika or cayenne pepper for extra flavor.

Cook:
- Cook the succotash over medium heat for about 8-10 minutes or until the vegetables are tender, stirring occasionally.

Garnish (Optional):
- Garnish with fresh chopped parsley for a burst of freshness.

Serve:
- Serve the succotash as a side dish alongside your favorite main course.

Optional Tips:

- You can customize succotash by adding other vegetables such as cherry tomatoes, zucchini, or bell peppers.
- For a Southern twist, you can include bacon or ham for added flavor.
- Feel free to experiment with herbs and spices like thyme, smoked paprika, or cumin to enhance the taste.

Succotash is a versatile and colorful dish that can be enjoyed as a side dish or even as a light vegetarian main course. Its simplicity and flexibility make it a popular and comforting addition to many tables.

Pumpkin Bisque

Ingredients:

- 2 tablespoons unsalted butter
- 1 onion, chopped
- 2 cloves garlic, minced
- 4 cups pumpkin puree (canned or homemade)
- 4 cups vegetable or chicken broth
- 1 cup apple cider or apple juice
- 1 teaspoon ground cinnamon
- 1/2 teaspoon ground nutmeg
- 1/4 teaspoon ground ginger
- 1/4 teaspoon ground cloves
- Salt and black pepper, to taste
- 1 cup heavy cream or coconut milk
- Toasted pumpkin seeds (pepitas) for garnish (optional)
- Fresh parsley or chives for garnish (optional)

Instructions:

Sauté Onion and Garlic:
- In a large pot, melt the butter over medium heat. Add chopped onions and sauté until they become translucent. Add minced garlic and cook for an additional minute.

Add Pumpkin and Spices:
- Stir in the pumpkin puree, ground cinnamon, nutmeg, ginger, and cloves. Mix well to combine the ingredients.

Pour in Liquids:
- Pour in the vegetable or chicken broth and apple cider. Season with salt and black pepper to taste. Stir to combine.

Simmer:
- Allow the mixture to come to a simmer. Reduce the heat to low, cover the pot, and let it simmer for about 15-20 minutes to allow the flavors to meld.

Blend:
- Using an immersion blender, blend the soup until smooth. Alternatively, carefully transfer the soup in batches to a blender and blend until smooth. Be cautious when blending hot liquids.

Add Cream:

- Return the blended soup to the pot if needed. Stir in the heavy cream or coconut milk and warm the soup over low heat.

Adjust Seasoning:
- Taste the bisque and adjust the seasoning, adding more salt or spices if necessary.

Serve:
- Ladle the Pumpkin Bisque into bowls. Garnish with toasted pumpkin seeds and fresh parsley or chives if desired.

Enjoy:
- Serve the Pumpkin Bisque hot and enjoy this comforting fall soup.

Optional Tips:

- For an extra layer of flavor, you can roast the pumpkin before pureeing it.
- Adjust the consistency of the bisque by adding more broth or cream according to your preference.
- Drizzle a little extra cream or a dollop of sour cream on top before serving for added richness.

Pumpkin Bisque is a delightful soup that captures the essence of autumn with its warm and comforting flavors. It's perfect for cozy evenings or as a starter for holiday meals.

New England Style Pancakes

Ingredients:

- 1 cup all-purpose flour
- 2 tablespoons sugar
- 1 teaspoon baking powder
- 1/2 teaspoon baking soda
- 1/4 teaspoon salt
- 3/4 cup buttermilk
- 1/4 cup milk
- 1 large egg
- 2 tablespoons unsalted butter, melted
- Cooking spray or additional butter for the griddle

Instructions:

Preheat Griddle or Pan:
- Preheat a griddle or non-stick pan over medium heat.

Mix Dry Ingredients:
- In a large bowl, whisk together the flour, sugar, baking powder, baking soda, and salt.

Combine Wet Ingredients:
- In another bowl, whisk together the buttermilk, milk, egg, and melted butter.

Combine Mixtures:
- Pour the wet ingredients into the dry ingredients and stir until just combined. The batter should be a bit lumpy.

Prep the Griddle:
- Lightly grease the griddle or pan with cooking spray or a small amount of butter.

Cook Pancakes:
- Pour 1/4 cup of batter for each pancake onto the griddle. Cook until bubbles form on the surface, then flip and cook until the other side is golden brown.

Keep Warm:
- Transfer the cooked pancakes to a warm oven while you cook the remaining batter.

Serve:
- Serve the New England-style pancakes with your favorite toppings, such as maple syrup, fresh fruit, or whipped cream.

Optional Tips:

- For added flavor, you can include a dash of vanilla extract or a sprinkle of cinnamon in the batter.
- Experiment with different toppings like blueberries, chocolate chips, or chopped nuts.
- If you don't have buttermilk, you can make a buttermilk substitute by adding 1 tablespoon of vinegar or lemon juice to 1 cup of milk and letting it sit for a few minutes.

Enjoy these classic New England-style pancakes for a delicious and comforting breakfast!

Clam and Corn Chowder

Ingredients:

- 4 slices bacon, chopped
- 1 onion, finely chopped
- 2 cloves garlic, minced
- 2 tablespoons all-purpose flour
- 3 cups fresh or frozen corn kernels
- 2 cups potatoes, peeled and diced
- 2 cups chicken or vegetable broth
- 1 cup clam juice (from canned clams)
- 2 cups milk
- 2 cans (6.5 ounces each) chopped clams, drained
- Salt and black pepper, to taste
- 1/2 teaspoon dried thyme
- 1 bay leaf
- 1 cup heavy cream (optional)
- Fresh parsley, chopped, for garnish

Instructions:

Cook Bacon:
- In a large pot or Dutch oven, cook the chopped bacon over medium heat until it becomes crispy. Remove some of the bacon for garnish if desired, leaving some in the pot for flavor.

Sauté Onion and Garlic:
- Add the finely chopped onion to the pot and sauté until it becomes translucent. Add minced garlic and cook for an additional minute.

Stir in Flour:
- Sprinkle the flour over the onion and garlic, stirring constantly to create a roux. Cook for 2-3 minutes to eliminate the raw flour taste.

Add Vegetables:
- Stir in the corn and diced potatoes, coating them with the roux.

Pour in Liquids:
- Pour in the chicken or vegetable broth, clam juice, and milk. Add the drained chopped clams. Stir to combine.

Season and Simmer:

- Season the chowder with salt, black pepper, dried thyme, and add the bay leaf. Bring the mixture to a simmer, then reduce the heat to low. Cover and let it simmer for about 15-20 minutes or until the potatoes are tender.

Add Cream (Optional):
- If using heavy cream, stir it in at this stage to add richness to the chowder. Adjust the seasoning if needed.

Serve:
- Ladle the Clam and Corn Chowder into bowls, garnish with the reserved crispy bacon and chopped parsley.

Enjoy:
- Serve the chowder hot and enjoy this comforting and flavorful soup!

Optional Tips:

- For added depth of flavor, you can include a pinch of Old Bay seasoning or a dash of hot sauce.
- If using fresh clams, steam them separately and add the clam meat to the chowder, discarding any shells.
- Adjust the thickness of the chowder by adding more broth or milk according to your preference.

This Clam and Corn Chowder is a delicious and hearty soup that makes for a satisfying meal, especially during colder months.

Cranberry Glazed Ham

Ingredients:

- 1 fully cooked ham (bone-in or boneless, about 6-8 pounds)
- 1 cup whole berry cranberry sauce
- 1/2 cup orange juice
- 1/2 cup brown sugar
- 2 tablespoons Dijon mustard
- 1 teaspoon ground cinnamon
- 1/2 teaspoon ground cloves
- 1/4 teaspoon ground nutmeg

Instructions:

Preheat Oven:
- Preheat your oven to 325°F (163°C).

Prepare Ham:
- Place the ham in a roasting pan, fat side up. If the ham has a thick skin or rind, you can score it in a diamond pattern with a sharp knife.

Mix Glaze:
- In a saucepan over medium heat, combine cranberry sauce, orange juice, brown sugar, Dijon mustard, ground cinnamon, ground cloves, and ground nutmeg. Stir well and let it simmer for about 5-7 minutes, or until the mixture thickens slightly.

Brush Glaze:
- Brush a generous amount of the cranberry glaze over the entire surface of the ham. Make sure to get the glaze into the score marks if you've scored the ham.

Bake:
- Bake the ham in the preheated oven, uncovered, for about 15-20 minutes per pound. Baste the ham with the cranberry glaze every 30 minutes to keep it moist and flavorful.

Check Internal Temperature:
- Use a meat thermometer to check the internal temperature of the ham. The ham is done when it reaches an internal temperature of 140°F (60°C) for pre-cooked hams or 145°F (63°C) for raw hams.

Rest and Serve:

- Once the ham is cooked, remove it from the oven, cover it loosely with aluminum foil, and let it rest for about 15 minutes before slicing.

Slice and Serve:
- Slice the ham and serve it with any remaining cranberry glaze on the side.

Optional Tips:

- If you want a more caramelized and crispy exterior, you can broil the ham for a few minutes at the end of the cooking time.
- Garnish the serving platter with fresh cranberries, orange slices, or herbs for a festive presentation.
- You can use the leftover cranberry glaze as a sauce for serving.

This Cranberry Glazed Ham is a perfect centerpiece for holiday meals or special occasions, bringing a burst of festive flavors to your table.

Boston Cream Pie Cheesecake

Ingredients:

For the Crust:

- 1 1/2 cups graham cracker crumbs
- 1/4 cup unsalted butter, melted
- 2 tablespoons sugar

For the Cheesecake Filling:

- 4 packages (8 ounces each) cream cheese, softened
- 1 cup sugar
- 4 large eggs
- 1 teaspoon vanilla extract
- 1/2 cup sour cream
- 1/2 cup all-purpose flour

For the Pastry Cream Layer:

- 2 cups whole milk
- 1/2 cup granulated sugar
- 1/4 cup cornstarch
- 1/4 teaspoon salt
- 4 large egg yolks
- 2 tablespoons unsalted butter
- 2 teaspoons vanilla extract

For the Chocolate Ganache:

- 1/2 cup heavy cream
- 4 ounces semi-sweet chocolate, finely chopped

Instructions:

For the Crust:

  Preheat Oven:
  - Preheat your oven to 325°F (163°C).

Prepare Pan:
- Grease a 9-inch springform pan.

Make Crust:
- In a bowl, combine graham cracker crumbs, melted butter, and sugar. Press the mixture into the bottom of the prepared pan to form the crust.

Bake:
- Bake the crust for about 10 minutes. Remove from the oven and let it cool while you prepare the cheesecake filling.

For the Cheesecake Filling:

Beat Cream Cheese:
- In a large bowl, beat the softened cream cheese until smooth.

Add Sugar and Eggs:
- Add sugar and beat until well combined. Add the eggs one at a time, beating well after each addition.

Add Vanilla, Sour Cream, and Flour:
- Mix in the vanilla extract, sour cream, and flour until the batter is smooth.

Pour Over Crust:
- Pour the cheesecake batter over the prepared crust in the springform pan.

Bake:
- Bake the cheesecake in the preheated oven for about 50-60 minutes, or until the center is set and the top is lightly browned.

Cool:
- Allow the cheesecake to cool in the pan, then refrigerate for at least 4 hours or overnight.

For the Pastry Cream Layer:

Prepare Pastry Cream:
- In a saucepan, heat the milk until it is steaming but not boiling. In a separate bowl, whisk together sugar, cornstarch, salt, and egg yolks.

Temper Eggs:
- Gradually whisk the hot milk into the egg mixture to temper the eggs. Return the mixture to the saucepan.

Cook:
- Cook over medium heat, stirring constantly, until the mixture thickens. Remove from heat and stir in butter and vanilla extract.

Cool:

- Let the pastry cream cool completely.

Spread Over Cheesecake:
- Spread the cooled pastry cream over the chilled cheesecake.

For the Chocolate Ganache:

Heat Cream:
- In a small saucepan, heat the heavy cream until it just starts to simmer.

Pour Over Chocolate:
- Pour the hot cream over the finely chopped chocolate. Let it sit for a minute, then stir until smooth.

Pour Over Pastry Cream:
- Pour the chocolate ganache over the pastry cream layer.

Chill:
- Return the Boston Cream Pie Cheesecake to the refrigerator to allow the chocolate ganache to set.

Serve:
- Once set, run a knife around the edge of the springform pan, release the sides, and transfer the cheesecake to a serving plate.

Slice and Enjoy:
- Slice and enjoy this decadent Boston Cream Pie Cheesecake!

This Boston Cream Pie Cheesecake is a show-stopping dessert that combines the best elements of a classic Boston Cream Pie and a rich cheesecake. Perfect for special occasions or when you want to impress your guests!

Lobster Newberg

Ingredients:

- 2 lobsters (about 1 1/2 to 2 pounds each), cooked and meat removed from the shells
- 1/4 cup unsalted butter
- 1/4 cup all-purpose flour
- 1 cup heavy cream
- 1/4 cup dry white wine
- 3 tablespoons brandy
- 4 large egg yolks
- Salt and white pepper, to taste
- Pinch of cayenne pepper (optional)
- Toast points or puff pastry shells, for serving
- Chopped fresh parsley, for garnish

Instructions:

Prepare Lobster Meat:
- Cut the lobster meat into bite-sized pieces. Set aside.

Make Roux:
- In a saucepan over medium heat, melt the butter. Stir in the flour to create a roux. Cook the roux for a couple of minutes until it's lightly golden, but be careful not to let it brown too much.

Add Cream and Wine:
- Gradually whisk in the heavy cream and white wine, stirring continuously to avoid lumps. Bring the mixture to a gentle simmer.

Add Brandy:
- Stir in the brandy and continue to simmer for a few more minutes to cook off the alcohol.

Temper Egg Yolks:
- In a separate bowl, beat the egg yolks. Slowly pour a small amount of the hot cream mixture into the beaten egg yolks, whisking constantly to temper the eggs.

Combine Mixtures:
- Gradually add the egg yolk mixture back into the saucepan, whisking constantly to combine. Cook the sauce over low heat, stirring

continuously, until it thickens. Be cautious not to let it boil to prevent curdling.

Season:
- Season the sauce with salt, white pepper, and a pinch of cayenne pepper if desired. Adjust the seasoning to your taste.

Add Lobster Meat:
- Gently fold in the lobster meat, making sure it is well coated with the sauce. Cook for a few more minutes until the lobster is heated through.

Serve:
- Serve Lobster Newberg over toast points or in puff pastry shells. Garnish with chopped fresh parsley.

Optional Tips:

- You can add a touch of lemon juice or nutmeg for extra flavor.
- Adjust the thickness of the sauce by adding more cream if needed.
- Some variations include the addition of mushrooms or shallots for added depth.

Lobster Newberg is a luxurious and elegant dish that is perfect for special occasions or when you want to treat yourself to a decadent seafood meal.

www.ingramcontent.com/pod-product-compliance
Lightning Source LLC
LaVergne TN
LVHW081551060526
838201LV00054B/1850